The Political Economy of Protection

FUNDAMENTALS OF PURE AND APPLIED ECONOMICS

Fundamentals of Pure and Applied Economics is an international series of titles divided by discipline into sections. A list of sections and their editors and of published titles may be found at the back of this volume.

The Political Economy of Protection

Arye L. Hillman
Bar-Ilan University, Israel

A volume in the International Trade section

edited by

Murray Kemp
University of New South Wales, Australia

harwood academic publishers
Switzerland · Australia · Belgium · France · Germany ·
Great Britain · India · Japan · Malaysia · Netherlands ·
Russia · Singapore · USA

First published 1989
Second printing 1994

Harwood Academic Publishers
Poststrasse 22
7000 Chur, Switzerland

Library of Congress Cataloging-in-Publication Data

Hillman, Arye L.
   The political economy of protection/Arye L. Hillman.
   p.   cm.—(Fundamentals of pure and applied economics: v.
32. International trade section.)
   Bibliography: p.
   Includes index.
   ISBN 3-7186-4873-3
   1. Protectionism.   2. Commercial policy.   3. International trade.
I. Title.   II. Series: Fundamentals of pure and applied economics;
v. 32.   III. Series: Fundamentals of pure and applied economics.
International trade section.
HF 1713.H63   1989
382.7′3—dc19
                                        88-39635
                                        CIP

Contents

Introduction to the Series

Drawing on a personal network, an economist can still relatively easily stay well informed in the narrow field in which he works, but to keep up with the development of economics as a whole is a much more formidable challenge. Economists are confronted with difficulties associated with the rapid development of their discipline. There is a risk of "balkanization" in economics, which may not be favorable to its development.

Fundamentals of Pure and Applied Economics has been created to meet this problem. The discipline of economics has been subdivided into sections (listed inside). These sections include short books, each surveying the state of the art in a given area.

Each book starts with the basic elements and goes as far as the most advanced results. Each should be useful to professors needing material for lectures, to graduate students looking for a global view of a particular subject, to professional economists wishing to keep up with the development of their science, and to researchers seeking convenient information on questions that incidentally appear in their work.

Each book is thus a presentation of the state of the art in a particular field rather than a step-by-step analysis of the development of the literature. Each is a high-level presentation but accessible to anyone with a solid background in economics, whether engaged in business, government, international organizations, teaching, or research in related fields.

Three aspects of *Fundamentals of Pure and Applied Economics* should be emphasized:

—First, the project covers the whole field of economics, not only theoretical or mathematical economics.

—Second, the project is open-ended and the number of books is not predetermined. If new interesting areas appear, they will generate additional books.

—Last, all the books making up each section will later be grouped to constitute one or several volumes of an Encyclopedia of Economics.

The editors of the sections are outstanding economists who have selected as authors for the series some of the finest specialists in the world.

J. Lesourne   *H. Sonnenschein*

The Political Economy of Protection

ARYE L. HILLMAN

Bar-Ilan University, Israel

INTRODUCTION: THE EFFICIENCY OF FREE TRADE AND THE PREVALENCE OF PROTECTION

The welfare theorems of the theory of international trade imply with some qualification that free trade maximizes a country's national income and permits the achievement of maximal aggregate consumption possibilities. It is apparent, however, that the efficiency-based theorems on the optimality of free trade do not always guide governments in their conduct of trade policy. Protectionist outcomes abound.

The neo-classical theorems that underlie the case for free trade are propositions about efficiency and aggregate welfare. The theorems indicate that, given sufficient information, compensating lump-sum transfers can ensure that a policy of free trade is in the self-interest of every individual in an economy. However, in the absence of compensatory transfers or other income adjustments, there may be disagreement regarding the course that different individuals wish trade policy to take. For a country's trade policy affects the domestic distribution of income. As such, the considerations bearing upon the conduct of a country's trade policy extend beyond efficiency issues to encompass income distribution concerns.

The body of literature that falls under the heading of the political economy of protection focuses on the role of income-distribution motives in explaining the conduct of trade policy. The political-economy literature departs from a tradition in international trade theory that has stressed the gains from international trade which accrue to a country in aggregate and the efficiency losses

1

incurred by an economy as a whole as the consequence of different types of trade policies.

This latter tradition has also suggested explanations for protectionist policies. The optimum-tariff and infant-industry arguments constitute the classical grounds for protection. The case for an optimum tariff is based on the application of a country's market power in the international market to improve its terms of trade. The argument is however weakened by the potential for foreign retaliation (although the tariff-initiating economy may possibly gain notwithstanding retaliation). The infant-industry argument has also been observed to be compromised by a number of considerations; it is in particular well-established that protection is by no means the appropriate means of internalizing the learning externalities associated with infant industries.

Some other explanations for departure from free trade have been proposed within the framework of the traditional theory. One set of arguments has to do with issues relating to national defense, self-sufficiency, and the costs of disruption of import supply. There are additionally a number of 'second-best' arguments for protection associated with the presence of 'distortions' or inefficiencies in the functioning of domestic markets. The 'second-best' arguments acknowledge the desirability of free trade, but assume circumstances where the 'first-best' outcome (free trade) is not attainable because of constraints on policy options. Departure from free trade therefore yields an outcome which is 'second-best' (although first-best when viewed in terms of the prespecified policy options). Various strategic arguments have also been suggested for trade intervention when international trade is undertaken by oligopolistic firms. The latter arguments (which have been subjected to reservations in the literature) propose a role for government as intervening in support of the strategic position (or to provide a credible commitment for strategic policies) of domestic firms confronting foreign rivals.

These various above arguments qualify the efficiency case for free trade. For example, a government confronted with uncertainty regarding continued trading opportunities might, in the presence of adjustment costs in production (which for some reason are not internalized by domestic producers) be advised to impose a protective tariff on imports of goods subject to trade disruption; or a government confronting monopoly in the domestic labor market might be demonstrated to maximize an index of aggregate national welfare by adopting a 'second-best' policy that restricts trade (the 'first-best' policy would retain free trade but eliminate the source of domestic monopoly power). However, while such arguments can in principle be drawn upon to explain why departures from free trade might be recommended in particular circumstances, there is little compelling evidence on which to rest a claim that these different efficiency-based qualifications individually or taken together explain either the opportunities for protection provided by the national trade laws of the developed countries or the prevalence of protectionist policies. There is however a considerable body of evidence supportive of the proposition that protectionist policies emanate primarily from the domestic political process and reflect domestic income distribution concerns. The political-economy perspective on international trade policy emphasizes the role of these income-distribution concerns in the formulation of trade policy and stresses that the many instances of observed departure from free trade have less to do with optimum-tariff, infant-industry, second-best, national-defense and strategic oligopolistic considerations than with the resolution via the political mechanism of the domestic conflict between the gainers and losers from protection.

Endogenous protection

The theory of the political economy of protection views trade policy as endogenously determined. To this end, self-interested behavior is imputed to policymakers (or potential policymakers, as candidates for political office), just as consumers and producers in neoçlassical economic theory are assumed to act in accord with their perceived self-interest. Trade policy is viewed as determined jointly by (i) the objectives of policymakers, (ii) the influence over policy exerted by the gainers and losers from protectionist proposals, and (iii) the institutional setting governing the interaction between policymakers and the gainers and losers from protection. In contrast with this endogenous policy vantage, the more traditional approach to the theory of international trade has taken the presence of tariffs, quotas, and other trade barriers as given, and has not enquired as to how and why such trade barriers come about and remain sustained.

The theory of the political economy of protection addresses questions such as how observed trade barriers have emerged, why different industries have achieved different levels of protection, and why protection takes different forms in different instances.

The institutional setting

The endogenous determination of trade policy as described in this monograph assumes an institutional setting wherein individuals and coalitions of interested parties are free to seek to influence policy outcomes via the democratic process. This process may be direct democracy or representative democracy. There are therefore evident limitations on the applicability of the theory to explanations of policy determination within the broader community of nations. With only limited exceptions (for example, Australia, India, Israel, Japan, New Zealand, Sri Lanka) has the precondition of a democratic political environment been consistently satisfied in post World-War II years outside of North America and Western Europe.

The free-trade presumption

Although some individuals may gain and others may lose from protection, there is nonetheless a strong presumption favoring free-trade outcomes. This presumption rests on the Coase Theorem. The Theorem states that in the absence of inhibiting transactions costs Pareto-efficient outcomes will obtain independently of property rights. We can here consider the assignment of rights (by whatever process) to the determination of a country's trade policy.

Consider a competitive pure exchange economy confronting given world prices. Let agents in the economy be asymmetrically endowed with given quantities of tradeable commodities and in the absence of opportunities to engage in international trade let the goods be traded domestically at domestic market-clearing prices. In general, international market prices will differ from domestic market-clearing prices, so the opportunity to engage in international trade will yield gains to the economy in aggregate relative to autarky. However, in the absence of compensatory transfers, international trade will result in welfare losses for some domestic agents, since in the course of the move from autarky to free trade some agents will have experienced a deterioration in the terms at which they individually engage in exchange.

Let the gainers from free trade have the discretion to determine trade policy. Given a choice between free trade and protection, they naturally enough choose free trade, since they gain by trading at international prices.

Alternatively, let policy discretion rest with the losers from free trade. Since free trade offers consumption possibilities that are in aggregate superior to those achievable via protection, the latter agents also maximize welfare by exercizing policy discretion to choose free trade, and then by applying their discretion to determine policy so as to share in or appropriate the gains from international trade.

Thus, everybody has an interest in the achievement of the efficient outcome attainable via free trade. There is simply more to share. Consistently with the Coase Theorem, the Pareto-efficient outcome (free trade) should thus obtain without regard for designation of the right to determine policy. Failure of the Coase Theorem is in this case as in other instances traced to transactions costs, here the costs of making the compensatory transfers that are necessary if free trade is to be unanimously preferred to protection. If a prerequisite for compensation is identification of the individual gainers and losers from free trade, and if such identification is excessively costly or is not feasible, the losers from free trade have an interest in seeking to secure the implementation of protectionist policies, even though in principle everybody could be better off under free trade.

The structure

The structure of this monograph is as follows. Section 1 reviews the predictions of international trade theory regarding identification of the gainers and losers from protection when no compensatory domestic transfers of income take place. Identification of gainers and losers permits a determination of the positions that individuals acting in their own self-interest will take regarding the conduct of trade policy. It is a maintained assumption throughout this monograph that compensating transfers from gainers from free trade to gainers from protection such as would facilitate adherence to free-trade policies do not take place.

Section 2 introduces the interests of gainers and losers from protection into a framework wherein political self-interest motives of policymakers underlie the conduct of trade policy. Policymakers are viewed as optimizing agents concerned with maximizing political support which derives from the gainers and losers from protectionist proposals. Motives of political self-interest in the conduct of trade policy are shown to be consistent with behavior by policymakers that has been linked to motives of social justice, or altruism, or social-welfare maximization. The protectionist response that maximizes political support is described when policymakers confront industries which are in decline because of import competition. Protectionist decisions deriving from the political-support motives of policymakers are also shown to underlie the possibility of sudden collapse of import-competing industries.

Section 3 describes the types of outcomes that could be envisaged, were trade policies determined in a system of direct democracy, where individuals could vote directly on the trade policy that they wished to have implemented.

Opportunities for direct voting on trade-policy issues are rarely present. Section 4 returns to the setting of section 2 where trade-policy decisions are at the discretion of political agents. The determination of trade policy is described in a system of representative democracy, where policy discretion is delegated to elected representatives. Various models are described wherein individuals pursuing their self interests seek to influence trade-policy decisions to their advantage.

Sections 5 and 6 are concerned with the valuation of the resources used in seeking to influence trade-policy outcomes. Here the emphasis is on efficiency, via the opportunity cost of using resources to achieve policy outcomes that change the distribution of income. In principle, the same resources could have used in ways that increase income rather than in attempts (successful or otherwise) to redistribute income, hence the potential efficiency loss. However, these resources are also used in self expression in a democratic system. Section 5 reviews a literature which has directed attention to the possibility that resources used in seeking to influence trade-policy decisions may have negative shadow prices. Section 6 adopts the perspective of a theory of contests wherein resources are allocated to contesting politically allocated prizes.

Section 7 considers the political choice of the instrument of protection. The considerations underlying policymakers' choice from among the various means of protection are reviewed. Section 8 introduces foreign interests into the political choice of the means of protection. A special role emerges for voluntary export restraints as the instrument of trade restriction.

Section 9 examines social-insurance or social-justice explanations for protection, and compares such explanations with the political self-interest perspective on the determination of trade policy.

Section 10 sets out the institutional aspects of the formulation of trade policy in the U.S. The manners in which protection can be sought and is granted in the United States are described, as are the links between national trade policy and the General Agreement on Tariffs and Trade.

Empirical studies are reviewed in Section 11. Evidence is presented from econometric analyses and case studies. The evidence presented in general confirms that the conduct of trade policy is principally explained by income-distribution considerations.

Section 12 contains concluding remarks, with observations on the role of policy recommendations in an environment of political competition.

Bibliographic notes

Proofs of the propositions on the gains from trade with lump-sum transfers are set out in Samuelson (1962) and Kemp (1962). Dixit and Norman (1980) propose a proof of the gains from trade without lump-sum transfers; see also the interchange between Kemp and Wan (1986) and Dixit and Norman (1986). For a critique of the infant-industry argument for protection, see Baldwin (1969). Cheng (1987) reviews arguments for self-sufficiency in international trade. The theory of distortions and second-best arguments underlying trade policy is set out in Bhagwati (1971). On rational behavior and political motives, see Downs (1957), Buchanan and Tullock (1962). On strategic trade policy, see Krugman (ed.) (1987); for reservations, see Grossman and Richardson (1985), Dixit (1987). The Coase Theorem appears in Coase (1960). The work of Baldwin (for example, Baldwin, 1976, 1982, 1985) stresses the centrality of the role of political-economy considerations in explaining developed countries' trade policies.

1. IDENTIFYING THE GAINERS AND LOSERS FROM PROTECTION

Traditional general equilibrium international trade theory frames its conclusions within the setting of one of three models; the Ricardian or classical model wherein a single intersectorally mobile homogeneous factor (usually designated labor) is the sole factor of production; the Heckscher–Ohlin model which views the economy as endowed with at least two intersectorally mobile factors; and a model which allows for the presence of industry-specific as well as intersectorally mobile factors. In the single-factor Ricardian model, since there is but one source of income (from labor services) for all individuals in an economy, everybody gains from free trade and loses from protection. Thus no domestic coalitions arise that might seek to direct political activity at effecting a departure from free trade. However, the more structurally complex Heckscher–Ohlin and specific-factors settings identify gainers and losers from protection and point to coalitions that have conflicting interests regarding trade policy.

1.1. The Stolper–Samuelson Theorem

In the Heckscher–Ohlin model the Ricardian consensus among factor owners in favor of free trade disappears because of the presence of at least one more intersectorally mobile factor. Call this factor capital, and suppose that individuals derive their incomes from undiversified claims to either capital or labor. A conflict between factor owners with regard to trade policy then arises via the link between relative output prices and real factor returns. In a competitive economy, with two goods and two factors, the lines are simply drawn. Rule out the Metzler paradox: that is, protection necessarily increases the domestic relative price of an economy's import-competing good. The Stolper–Samuelson Theorem then states that protection increases the real income of owners of the economy's relatively scarce factor at the expense of owners of the relatively abundant factor who find that their real incomes have fallen. There are deadweight costs of protection. But the deadweight costs are borne by owners of the economy's relatively abundant factor. Real incomes of owners of the economy's relatively scarce factor increase, even though in aggregate real income has declined because of the departure from free trade.

International trade in goods in the Heckscher–Ohlin model translates directly into international exchange of factor services. The Stolper–Samuelson Theorem reveals how owners of the economy's relatively scarce factor gain when protection inhibits the import of competing foreign factor services embodied in the economy's imports.

Extension to encompass many goods produced by two factors does not affect the basic Stolper–Samuelson result. Protection of an import-competing good increases the real return of one factor at the expense of the second. Owners of the economy's relatively scarce factor therefore retain the incentive to seek protection for the import-competing sector.

However, the effectiveness of the Stolper–Samuelson Theorem as a means of predicting gainers and losers from protection diminishes somewhat when many goods are produced by many factors. A complete generalization of the two-good/two-factor Theorem requires stringent restrictions on production technologies. With no restrictions on technologies and with any number of goods and factors, protection of a good lowers the real income of some factor and raises that of another, provided that the protected good was domestically produced in the initial equilibrium and inputs employed in production of that good all had alternative domestic employment opportunities. However, a factor cannot conversely be assured of finding some good to which its real income is unambiguously tied. Some links do emerge. If the number of factors is equal to the number of goods, every factor will be able to identify a good which is a "natural adversary", in the sense that an increase in the relative price of that good will unambiguously lower the factor's real income. There need not exist a "natural friend." However, when allowance is made for expenditure patterns, each factor owner can increase his real income by securing a relative price increase for some good.

One need not however seek precise associations between the real incomes of particular factors and relative prices of goods in order to identify a factor owner's stance on trade policy. The Stolper–Samuelson Theorem holds in general terms in an average sense. With no restrictions placed on technologies and for any number of goods and factors, competitive cost minimization implies that protection of a good which is relatively intensive in the use of a factor will on average increase that factor's real income.

1.2. Specific factors

The Stopler–Samuelson Theorem identifies the gainers and losers from protection when individuals' incomes derive exclusively from undiversified claims of ownership over factors that are intersectorally mobile. Since intersectoral mobility implies that factors are not tied to an industry, but rather are indifferent in a competitive equilibrium between employment opportunities in different industries, the Theorem gives rise to factor-based coalitions. It is however industry-specific interests that in general are observed to be active in seeking protection. Industry-specific interests are associated with industry-specific factors. Returns to industry-specific factors consist of the residual (or rents) remaining after intersectorally mobile factors have been paid their competitively determined returns. Industry-specific factors therefore have a particular interest in seeking to influence trade policy, to protect or increase their rents.

A simple rendition of a model with specific factors is provided by considering two tradeable goods produced by competitive firms via neo-classical constant-returns-to-scale technologies $x_i = F^i(\bar{K}_i, L_i)$ where $\bar{K}_i$ $(i = 1, 2)$ is an inelastically supplied factor (capital) specific to industry i. The mobile factor L (labor) is inelastically supplied to the economy and is fully employed in the production of the two goods. In a diversified production equilibrium competition ensures that the value of the marginal product of labor in its alternative uses is equal to the nominal wage. Hence, denoting marginal products by subscripts,

$$PF_L^1 = w = F_L^2 \tag{1.1}$$

where w is the nominal wage and $P \equiv P_1/P_2$. Let good 1 be the import-competing good, and let this good be protected, so raising P. To restore labor-market equilibrium as expressed by (1.1), mobile labor exits sector 2 and enters sector 1. Given diminishing returns, F_L^1 falls and F_L^2 increases. These marginal products are respectively equal to the real wage of labor in terms of each good. Mobile labor thus loses from protection in terms of good 1 and gains in terms of good 2. A mobile-factor owner's consumption preferences therefore establish the factor's position on trade policy. In the absence of information on consumption preferences, the self-interested policy stance of a mobile factor is ambiguous. This outcome has been termed the 'neo-classical ambiguity'.

There is however no ambiguity in the determination of whether an owner of an industry-specific factor gains or loses from protection. Those individuals with claims to factors specific to the import-competing sector gain, and conversely those with claims to factors specific to the export sector lose. The gains and losses to owners of industry-specific factors follow readily from the technological complementarity of factor inputs implied by constant returns to scale—that is, $F_{KL}^i > 0$ $(i = 1, 2)$. F_K^1 increases when mobile labor enters the import-competing sector while F_K^2 declines as mobile labor exits the export sector. Protection therefore increases the real return to the factor specific to the import-competing sector, in terms of the protected good whose relative price has increased, and also therefore in terms of the export good whose relative price has fallen. In the export sector the return to the specific factor will conversely have declined in terms of either good.

This identification of the gainers and losers from protection extends readily to any number of goods. Factors specific to any industry have an interest in seeking protection for their industry, and only their industry, while opposing protection for any other industry. And whether a mobile factor gains or loses from protection of a particular import-competing industry remains without further qualifying information ambiguous.

A basis has however been proposed for a presumption that mobile factors will lose from protection. The presumption derives from a comparison of goods' relative shares in domestic production and consumption. When protection increases the relative price P_i of an import-competing good i, the nominal wage w increases by a proportionate amount given by $\hat{w} = \beta_i \hat{P_i}$, where $\beta_i = \xi_i \lambda_{Li}/\xi > 0$, ξ_i is the elasticity of demand for labor with respect to the real wage in sector i, ξ is the economy-wide average labor-demand elasticity, and λ_{Li} is the proportion of labor employed in sector i. Whether labor will have gained from this increase in the nominal wage depends on how good i figures in a wage-earner's consumption expenditure. Denoting by α_i the consumption share of good i, the wage-earner gains if sign$(\beta_i - \alpha_i)$ is positive and loses if sign$(\beta_i - \alpha_i)$ is negative. Since good i is imported, its consumption share in the economy exceeds its production share. That is, denoting the production share by θ_i, then $\alpha_i > \theta_i$. Let the latter inequality in particular hold for the consumption share of mobile labor. Now, define good i as unbiased with respect to labor if an increase in the relative price of good i increases labor's nominal return w in the same proportion as it on average increases other factor prices. This means that $\beta_i = \theta_i$. Hence sign$(\beta_i - \alpha_i)$ = sign$(\theta_i - \alpha_i) < 0$, in which case the mobile factor has lost as a consequence of protection. Since on the above definition goods are on average unbiased, on average the mobile labor loses from protection and hence has an interest in supporting a policy of free trade.

However, in a world of many goods, the magnitude of loss to mobile labor (or possibly gain) from protection of any one good will tend to be small, insofar as any one good makes up but a small share of a mobile factor's consumption expenditure.

1.3. Long and short-run interests

If intersectoral factor immobility is a short-run characteristic, the Heckscher–Ohlin and specific-factors models respectively identify factor owners' long and short-run interests in the conduct of a country's international trade policy. Long and short-run interests so defined can conflict.

Thus, in the two-good/two-factor setting, suppose that protection increases the relative price of the relatively capital-intensive good. Via the Stolper–Samuelson Theorem, domestic owners of capital then gain in the long run when all factors have had time to adjust to equate the values of marginal products across industries. In the short run, with capital sector-specific, owners of capital specific to the domestic import-competing industry gain and owners of capital specific to the export sector lose from protection. The latter factor owners accordingly confront an intertemporal conflict of interest in their stance on trade policy. They gain in the long run and lose in the short run. Mobile labor whose position is ambiguous in the short run necessarily loses from protection in the long run.

Alternatively, consider an economy wherein protection increases the relative price of the labor-intensive good. Mobile labor then gains in the long run. Owners of capital specific to the export sector lose in both the short and the long run. Owners of capital specific to the import-competing sector on the other hand confront the long-run/short-run conflict: protection is to their advantage in the short-run, but they lose in the long run.

The short-run perspective appears to dominate the determination of positions taken on trade policy. For in general, it is industries that seek protection, not coalitions of intersectorally mobile factor owners. Industry specificity as the basis for collective interest in the pursuit of protection is confirmed in empirical studies. Stephen Magee (1980) observed with limited exceptions that management and labor in an industry both adopted pro-protectionist positions in testimony before Congress on the 1974 Trade Act. Pugel and Walter (1985) studied the political activities of a number of large corporations throughout the 1970s and observed that positions taken on trade policy reflected a corporation's self-interest in seeking protection from competitive imports or supporting export-promoting policies. Gene Grossman and James Levinsohn (1987) studied the relationship between prices of competitive imports and stock-market returns to capital in a number of U.S import-competing industries. Increased import prices were associated with above-normal stock market returns in the industries studied. The magnitude of the returns suggested that capital was highly sector-specific in five out of the six industries studied.

The indications are thus that coalitions seeking to influence trade policy form along industry lines rather than being factor-based. Since individuals' short-run interests are prominent in determining the stances taken on protection, the specific-factors rather than the Heckscher-Ohlin setting appears more appropriate for policy-relevant identification of the interests seeking to influence trade policy.

However, the basic specific-factors model does not appear to suffice for identifying individuals' trade-policy positions. Labor rarely appears to satisfy the condition characterizing complete factor mobility, of being indifferent between staying on in employment in an industry and exiting to seek employment elsewhere.

1.4. Imperfectly substitutable factors

Even labor which is ostensibly intersectorally mobile often takes an industry-specific position. Of course, an individual may be intersectorally mobile in terms of his allocation of time while his embodied human capital may be industry-specific. Different individuals' human capital may further exhibit different degrees of industry specifity. It therefore becomes necessary to distinguish between a factor's intersectoral mobility and the income differential associated with the factor's alternative employment opportunities.

The specific-factors model can be amended to encompass mobile factors with different productivities in alternative employment. Different productivities in alternative employment implies that mobile factors are imperfectly substitutable across industries.

Let two goods be competitively produced via neo-classical constant-returns-to-scale technologies, $x_i = F^i[\bar{K}_i, L_i]$, $i = 1, 2$. In efficiency terms, mobile labor exhibits differential factor productivities in employment in the two sectors as expressed in the transformation function

$$L_2 = H(L_1), \qquad H' < 0, \qquad H'' < 0. \qquad (1.2)$$

The elasticity of this function $\sigma \equiv H'/L_1 H'' > 0$ measures the extent to which labor is substitutable at the margin in alternative employment. In the standard specific-factors model, labor is perfectly substitutable, yielding the limiting case of $\sigma = \infty$.

This model differs from the standard specific-factors setting only in the specification of imperfect substitutability of the mobile factor as given by (1.2). Thus, the competitive labor market efficiently allocates labor and in each sector the wage per efficiency unit of labor equals the value of a factor's marginal product, with $PF_L^1 = w_1$ and $F_L^2 = w_2$, where $P \equiv P_1/P_2$. Consequently, relative labor demand is characterized by

$$w_1/w_2 = PF_L^1/F_L^2. \qquad (1.3)$$

Labor supply follows from maximization of labor income subject to the transformation function (1.2) to yield

$$w_1/w_2 = -H'(L_1), \tag{1.4}$$

which implies equalization of the return to labor in efficiency terms. Labor market equilibrium then entails

$$PF_L^1/F_L^2 = w_1/w_2 = -H'(L_1). \tag{1.5}$$

The effects of protection on factors' real incomes can be established using the equilibrium condition (1.5). Protection alters the equilibrium labor allocation, thereby changing factor returns. Thus, let good 1 be imported. Protection then increases the domestic relative price P. From (1.5) it follows that

$$\hat{L}_1 = \beta \hat{P}/\Delta > 0 \tag{1.6}$$

where a circumflex denotes proportional change, $\beta = \lambda_{L1}\xi_1\xi_2 > 0$, $\Delta = (\beta/\sigma) - \lambda_{L1}\xi_1 - \lambda_{L2}\xi_2$, λ_{Li} is the share of labor in output of good i, and $\xi_i = F_L^i/L_iF_{LL}^i$ is the elasticity of demand for labor in industry i. Since $\hat{L}_1 > 0$, it follows that $\hat{L}_2 < 0$; mobile labor exits the export industry and enters the protected import-competing industry.

The intersectoral reallocation of labor affects the returns to labor in the two industries as follows:

$$\hat{w}_1 = \eta_1 \hat{P} \tag{1.7}$$

$$(\hat{w}_1 - \hat{w}_2) = \hat{L}_1/\sigma = \beta \hat{P}/\sigma\Delta \tag{1.8}$$

$$\hat{w}_2 = \eta_2 \hat{P} \tag{1.9}$$

where $\eta_1 \equiv [(\beta/\sigma) - \lambda_{L1}\xi_1]/\Delta$, $\eta_2 = -\lambda_{L2}\xi_1/\Delta = \eta_1 - \beta/\sigma\Delta$.

Return now to the limiting case of perfect substitutability of the mobile factor between the two industries; with $\sigma = \infty$ it follows that $\eta_1 = \eta_2 = \eta$ where $0 < \eta < 1$. Therefore

$$\hat{w}_1 = \hat{w}_2 = \eta \hat{P}, \tag{1.10}$$

indicating that the real wage has risen in terms of good 1 and fallen in terms of good 2 (the neo-classical ambiguity again). But importantly there is no conflict of interest with regard to trade policy between mobile factors employed in the two sectors.

Now let labor be completely immobile between sectors, i.e., a specific factor. In this limiting case $\sigma = 0$. Since

$$\lim_{\sigma \to 0} \frac{\beta}{\sigma\Delta} = \beta/[\beta/\sigma - \lambda_{L1}\xi_1 - \lambda_{L2}\xi_2]\sigma = 1, \qquad (1.11)$$

it follows from (1.8) that

$$\hat{w}_1 - \hat{w}_2 = \hat{P}. \qquad (1.12)$$

A conflict of interest with regard to trade policy has now emerged between labor employed in different sectors. The degree of conflict is measured directly by the magnitude of the relative price change $\hat{P}$.

In the intermediate case of imperfect factor substitutability, $0 < \sigma < \infty$ implies

$$\hat{w}_1 > \hat{w}_2. \qquad (1.13)$$

Labor employed in sector 1 therefore fares better than labor employed in sector 2 as a consequence of protection of the import-competing sector producing good 1. The neo-classical ambiguity is still present. For labor employed in either sector, the real wage declines in terms of good 1 and increases in terms of good 2.

Owners of industry-specific capital continue to gain or lose unambiguously from protection depending on whether capital is specific to the import-competing or export sector. Of course, as $\sigma \to 0$, the difference between sector-specific capital and mobile labor diminishes. In the limit with $\sigma = 0$, all factors are specific, and factor owners confront the same gain or loss from a change in trade policy depending on their industry association.

The important characterization provided by this amended version of the specific-factors model is that factors which are intersectorally mobile may support protection for the industry wherein they are employed, because of inframarginal rents due to different factor productivities in different sectors. The model can therefore explain the industry association of mobile factors and provides a theoretical basis for the observation that mobile factors constitute part of industry-specific coalitions seeking protection. As do industry-specific factors which have no other employment options, imperfectly substitutable mobile factors may have an incentive to seek protection for their industry to increase or protect their rents.

An alternative formulation of imperfect factor mobility retains the assumption that the mobile factor (labor) is perfectly substitutable between sectors. Capital however exhibits differential factor productivities between sectors and an efficiency loss is incurred when a unit of capital is transferred from one sector to another. This model allows formulation of the intermediate case between Heckscher–Ohlin where no efficiency loss is incurred in the course of intersectoral capital mobility and the specific-factors case of complete efficiency loss for capital (or complete industry specificity). Consequently the model yields gains and losses from protection to different factor owners that are combinations of the Stolper–Samuelson and specific-factors outcomes. The extent to which a factor owner benefits from or is harmed by protection depends as in Stolper–Samuelson on the relative factor intensities in production of the economy's export and import-competing goods, but also on the efficiency loss incurred by capital as a consequence of intersectoral relocation. In particular, because of the latter efficiency loss, the Stolper–Samuelson condition that the protected sector's output be relatively labor intensive is necessary, but no longer sufficient, for perfectly mobile labor to benefit unambiguously from protection.

1.5. Unemployment

Protection, other than altering domestic allocation of mobile factors and changing the rents of inelastically supplied factors, can also affect unemployment levels. The gainers and losers from protection are then identified in a setting that encompasses unemployment for some factors of production.

To portray the possibility of unemployment, consider an implicit-contract wage-bargaining context, where a union representing an industry's employees confronts representatives of employers. The distribution of the gains from protection, and whether there are at all gains to one of the parties, depends upon whether there is unemployment in equilibrium, and also upon the bargaining solution concept adopted.

We now focus on an industry rather than the economy at large. Denote industry profits as

$$\pi = R(P, L) - wL \qquad (1.14)$$

where $R(P, L)$ is the industry revenue function, w is the wage paid to homogeneous labor L, and P is the price of output. In a competitive industry, $R(P, L) = PF(L)$ where the price P is given to the firm.

Assume that unions maximize the expected income of members who are risk-neutral (although the subsequent conclusions remain unaltered if union members are risk-averse and unions maximize expected utility of members). Let N be the exogenously given total union membership and let $\theta = \theta(L/N)$ be the probability that a union member will be unemployed. Union members' expected income is

$$u = \theta w + (1 - \theta)r, \tag{1.15}$$

where r is a strictly positive reservation wage.

Outcomes here are established via cooperative bargaining theory. The first step in applying cooperative bargaining theory is to specify the Pareto frontier of the feasible set and the disagreement point. Maximizing π and holding u constant yields the efficiency condition

$$R_L - w + (w - r)\left(\frac{d\theta}{dL}\right)\left(\frac{L}{\theta}\right) = 0. \tag{1.16}$$

All contracts that are efficient from the point of view of the firm and the union must satisfy (1.16). If the two parties fail to reach an agreement, union members withdraw their labor from the firm and receive their reservation wage, in which case $u = r$. Assuming production is entirely shut down and the firm has no fixed costs, if no agreement is reached $\pi = 0$.

There are two cases to consider, characterized by whether there is unemployment in equilibrium. Suppose union membership equals or exceeds the firm's demand for labor, so $N \geq L$. In this case L union members are employed and $(N - L)$ are unemployed. Assuming all union members are equally likely to be laid off, $\theta(L/N) = L/N$. The second case is that where union members are fully employed and additional workers are sought by the firm, so $N \leq L$. With full employment, $\theta(L/N) = 1$.

In the presence of unemployment, since $\theta = L/N$, it follows that $(d\theta/dL)(L/\theta) = 1$ and the efficiency condition (1.18) reduces to

$$R_L = r. \tag{1.17}$$

This condition specifies the level of employment which maximizes the joint surplus available for distribution between the union and the firm, given by $N(u - r) + \pi = R - rL$. For any division of this surplus, both sides of course have an interest in maximizing the amount available for distribution.

How the gains from bargaining are to be shared in general depends on the solution concept adopted. However, in this instance, most of the solutions which have been proposed to the bargaining problem, including the Nash solution, imply the same wage equation,

$$w = \alpha(R/L) + (1 - \alpha)r, \qquad 0 < \alpha < 1. \qquad (1.18)$$

Bargaining solutions usually include an axiom of symmetry; that is, the outcome does not depend on the identification of the players, which implies that $\alpha = 1/2$. Nothing is lost by dropping symmetry and letting α be any constant parameter between zero and one.

Equations (1.17) and (1.18) imply that protection increases the domestic price of the industry's output and increases employment,

$$\frac{dL}{dP} = -\frac{F_L}{R_{LL}} > 0. \qquad (1.19)$$

However, the effect of protection on the wage received by union members is ambiguous and given by

$$\frac{dw}{dP} = (\alpha/L)\left\{ F + \frac{[(R/L) - R_L]F_L}{R_{LL}} \right\} \gtreqless 0. \qquad (1.20)$$

The first term inside the brackets reflects the direct effect of an increase in revenue on a worker's average product and is positive. The second term represents the effect of an increase in employment on a worker's average product, which is negative. In general, the net effect cannot be determined. (With a Cobb–Douglas technology, the net effect is zero.) Nevertheless, both the firm and union members unambiguously benefit from protection, since

$$d\pi/dP = (1 - \alpha)F > 0 \qquad (1.21)$$

$$du/dP = \alpha F/N > 0. \qquad (1.22)$$

Revenue increases by R_p of which the firm receives a proportion $(1 - \alpha)$ and the union receives a proportion α.

In contrast, consider the case in which the industry is expanding and the demand for labor exceeds current union membership, so that $N \leq L$. Union members then do not confront the risk of unemployment. Hence $\theta = 1$ and $d\theta/dL = 0$. The condition (1.16) that the contract be efficient is now

$$R_L = w. \tag{1.23}$$

Thus, when there is no cause for concern about possible unemployment of its members, the union has nothing to lose by letting employment be set at the level that maximizes profits.

With full employment, different solution concepts applied to the bargaining problem yield different wage equations. The Nash solution implies, as before, that $w = \alpha(R/L) + (1 - \alpha)r$. Also, as before, with the Nash solution, $dL/dP > 0$ and dw/dP is indeterminate. But now, it is no longer necessarily the case that the firm and the union share an interest in protection, since

$$d\pi/dP = (1 - \alpha)[F + (R_L - r)(dL/dP)] > 0, \tag{1.24}$$

$$du/dP = (dw/dP)N \gtreqless 0. \tag{1.25}$$

Since dw/dP is indeterminate, so is du/dP. The Nash solution reveals the effect of protection on workers' wages to be subject to countervailing forces. When union members not concerned about employment, the Nash solution implies that they have no special interest in and may possibly even oppose protection.

Another solution to the bargaining problem when utility and monetary payoffs are equal is the proportional solution. This solution is Pareto efficient, individually rational, invariant under transformation, homogeneous and monotonic if and only if it can be written in the form $(u - r)(1 - \alpha)N = \alpha\pi$. Since $u = w$ when $L \geq N$, this implies that

$$w = \frac{\alpha R + (1 - \alpha)rN}{\alpha L + (1 - \alpha)N}. \tag{1.26}$$

With the proportional solution, unlike the Nash case, both the firm and union members continue to benefit from protection when union members are fully employed, since

$$\frac{d\pi}{dP} = F + (R_L - w)\left(\frac{dL}{dP}\right) - L\left(\frac{dw}{dP}\right) = (1 - \alpha)F\frac{N}{\alpha L + (1 - \alpha)N} > 0,$$
$$(1.27)$$

$$\frac{du}{dP} = \left(\frac{dw}{dP}\right)N = (\alpha F/N)\frac{N}{\alpha L + (1 - \alpha)N} > 0. \qquad (1.28)$$

However, both the union and the firm benefit less than when some union members are unemployed. Compare (1.28) with (1.22). When $L > N$, the benefits to both the union and the firm are decreased by a factor of $N/[\alpha L + (1 - \alpha)N]$.

The Nash bargaining solution implies that the primary impact of protectionist policies is on employment rather than wages. When unemployment threatens, this is an important benefit from the union's point of view. But when union members are secure in their employment, the size of the firm's workforce is of little concern to them. On the basis of the Nash solution, only the firm unambiguously benefits from protection in circumstances where employment is growing and the demand for labor is greater than the union's membership.

The proportional solution implies that both union and firm share the benefits of protection whether employment is declining or growing. When there is unemployment, union members benefit from protection via higher employment. When union members are fully employed, they benefit from higher wages. But the gains from protection decline for both union members and the firm as the demand for labor exceeds the current union membership.

Both solutions have in common a reduction in the gains from protection when the workforce is growing. The same must be true for all solution concepts. Through collective bargaining, union members and firms form a coalition. While they are adversaries regarding the distribution of the payoffs, they are partners in the maximization of the surplus available for redistribution. When $N > L$, the employees' coalition exceeds the current industry workforce. Increases in the industry's demand for labor do not increase the coalition's size. However, when the demand for labor exceeds union membership, workers are hired who were initially outside the coalition. The gains from protection are then shared among the larger coalition. The Nash solution implies that the extension of benefits to new entrants comes largely or entirely at the expense of the share received by current employees, even to the extent that union members can be made worse off by an increase in demand for labor stemming from protection. The proportional solution implies that the gains received by both union members and the industry are diluted. In general, while the solutions differ on how the costs are apportioned, all imply a reduction of the benefits received by existing coalition members when increases in production lead to an expansion of the coalition's size.

The union and industry could jointly increase their benefits by excluding newly hired workers from union benefits. Union opposition to two-tiered wage contracts and other means of excluding new workers from the full benefits of union membership can be understood as a consequence of the union's need to maintain the source of its bargaining strength, which stems from its ability to inflict financial damage on firms by withdrawing the labor of its members. If $(L - N)$ workers were excluded from the union, profits in the event of a strike would not be $\pi = 0$ but $\pi = R(L - N) - r(L - N)$. The disagreement point would move in favor of employers. The exclusion of new workers from the union may therefore result in a reduction of union wages rather than an increase.

The effect of unemployment on protectionist demands in this model derives entirely from collective bargaining. If $\alpha = 0$ and workers receive the reservation wage, the impact of unemployment on the benefits from protection vanishes. However, the model is not limited to formal labor agreements. Whenever workers have acquired industry or firm-specific skills, there can be gap between workers' productivity in their current jobs and outside opportunities which creates rents to be shared and gives rise to implicit bargaining relationships. To the extent that employee-firm relationships consist of explicit or implicit bargaining rather than bidding for labor in Walrasian auction markets, the conclusions of the above bargaining model regarding the distribution of the gains from protection remain applicable.

1.6. Regional interests

The identification of the gainers and losers from protection can also have a regional vantage. If an industry is regionally important, the values of location-specific assets will tend to decline when the industry declines. Owners of factors which are in principle mobile may have significant holdings of location-specific assets, in particular, housing. Owners of mobile factors may therefore have in common with industry-specific factor owners an interest in supporting protection for a regionally concentrated industry. Hence, the more concentrated an industry is geographically, the greater pressure one might expect for protection in the face of import competition.

1.7. Monopoly rents

The Hecksher–Ohlin and specific-factors models use competitive general-equilibrium settings to identify gainers and losers from protection. Factor incomes change in accord with the Stolper–Samuelson Theorem as the consequence of protection. Or, in the specific-factors model, markets are competitive, but because of sector specificity some factors earn rents which are enhanced or diminished by changes in trade policy.

An alternative format to these competitive general-equilibrium settings focuses on monopoly power in domestic import-competing industries. Competitive imports available at given world prices restrain potential domestic monopoly power by inhibiting domestic firms from taking advantage of any domestic market power which they would otherwise have. Quotas and tariffs effect a separation between the domestic and world markets and thereby allow rents to be earned. A binding import quota facilitates domestic price discretion and thereby monopoly rents. Domestic quota holders also earn rents associated with the restriction of import supply. A tariff can also facilitate monopolistic price discretion. The gainers from protection are then the residual claimants to the monopoly rents and quota premia, the losers consumers who have been denied access to competitive supply at the world price of imports.

1.8. Foreign interests

A categorization of the various gainers and losers from protection includes foreign interests. Protectionist policies restrict foreigners' access to domestic markets and affect foreigners' profits. Thus, as do the various domestic interests, foreigners have an interest in the conduct of a country's international trade policy. The foreign interest is not necessarily in the pursuit of free-trade policies. An appropriately orchestrated contraction of trade, via "voluntary" export restraints or some other "orderly marketing arrangement" can increase the profits of foreign exporters, while at the same time benefitting domestic import-competing interests.

1.9. Bibliographic notes

The Stolper–Samuelson Theorem identifying the gainers and losers from protection was initially stated in Stolper and Samuelson (1941). The consequences for the Theorem of extension to many factors and many goods are set out in Ethier (1984). Jones and Scheinkman (1977) consider the properties of natural friends and adversaries. Cassing (1981) introduces the consequences of expenditure patterns. The specific-factors model is set out and investigated in Samuelson (1971), Jones (1971), Mayer (1974), Mussa (1974), Jones (1975) and Neary (1978). Ruffin and Jones (1977) investigate the "neo-classical ambiguity" and present the presumption that mobile factors lose from protection. Mussa (1982) and Baldwin (1984) introduce mobile factors with different productivities in the specific-factors model. Burgess (1980) provides the qualifications to the identification of gainers and losers in the specific-factors model required in the presence of inter-industry flows. Grossman (1983) combines Heckscher–Ohlin and specific-factor characteristics in a model of imperfect factor mobility. The model of unemployment, collective bargaining and the gains from protection is based on Wallerstein (1987). Cassing, McKeown and Ochs (1987) stress the identification of gainers and losers from protection in terms of regional interests. The possibility of mutual gains to foreign and domestic producers from the restriction of international trade is noted by Harris (1985), Krishna (1988), Eichenberger and Harper (1987), and Hillman and Ursprung (1988).

2. POLITICAL SELF-INTEREST MOTIVES AND PROTECTION

Protectionist decisions are the outcome of a political process that establishes legislated restrictions on international trade in particular goods, or specifies circumstances more broadly warranting trade intervention (for example, dumping or other trading practices designated as "unfair"). The formulation of the latter broad general rules within the context of GATT adherence is discussed in Section 10. We consider now trade policy directed at protecting a particular domestic import-competing industry and ask how policy-makers might respond in the formulation of trade policy to the conflict of interest between the individuals who gain and lose as the consequence of protection for the industry.

How discretion in the conduct of trade policy is exercised depends upon the motives of policymakers. Neoclassical economic theory imputes to individuals self-interested behavior. As consumers, individuals maximize utility; in their role as producers, individuals maximize profits. Consistency in the specification of behavioral motives of individuals whose livelihood derives from the attainment and maintenance of political office requires acknowledging the political self-interest motives of political agents. Thus discretion with respect to trade policy is predicted to be exercised in a manner which maximizes a political objective, such as the probability of reelection by incumbents. Political-support motives then underlie protectionist decisions.

The assignment of political self-interest objectives to political agents provides a basis for a theory of endogenous determination of trade policy. An alternative approach to endogenous trade policy assumes that policymakers make protectionist decisions based on motives of social justice, social welfare, or social insurance. This latter approach to endogenous trade policy is considered in Section 9, with a particular emphasis on the link between social insurance and protection. Until then, we assume that the behavior of political agents is explained by motives of political self-interest—and we assume that the behavior of economic agents in seeking to influence trade policy is predicated on their economic self-interest as gainers or losers from protectionist policies.

We begin with the declining industry, the natural candidate for assistance via protection on altruistic or social-justice grounds, and examine how political-support motives might influence protectionist decisions.

2.1. Political-support protectionist motives

Political-support protectionist motives can be formalized by portraying policymakers as pursuing their self interest by choosing trade policies to maximize probabilities of reelection subject to the political weights placed on the support of the gainers and losers from protection. The political-support model of industry regulation views regulated prices as determined in a manner which balances the marginal gain from the political support of industry interests who gain from an increase in industry profits against the marginal loss of political support from consumers confronting prices that have been increased by regulation. The regulator ensures that individual firms maintain the set price; industry/government collaboration is however subject to the political costs of consumer dissatisfaction. If consumers have some positive political weight, the politically optimal regulated price is less than the profit-maximizing price sought by producers. In addition to setting prices, the government in this model also ensures that entry into the industry does not occur. Entry which dissipates profits would eliminate the reason for producers' political support.

Entry into an industry which is in decline because of adverse shifts in comparative advantage is naturally unattractive, unless a protectionist response more than compensates for the losses to industry-specific factors due to industry decline. If entry does not occur, policymakers seeking political support from the declining industry confront a readily identifiable set of gainers from protection. Since the industry is in decline, gains to owners of industry-specific factors cannot be attributed to industry growth but are the evident consequence of protection.

Thus, just as declining industries are natural beneficiaries of protection explained as motivated by altruism or social justice, so they are natural candidates for protection explained in terms of motives of political support.

The political-support maximizing model of regulation of industry provides, with some modification, a frame of reference appropriate for describing self-interested choice of trade intervention. With the general-equilibrium specific-factors model as background, let π represent the real return to factors specific to a declining industry and denote by P the domestic relative price of the industry's output. Protection which increases P accordingly yields a gain to factors specific to the industry via an increase in π, and factors specific to all other industries lose. Hence, there are well-identified gainers and losers from protection.

In an application to trade policy, the free-trade equilibrium and the world price of the import-competing industry's output are reference points for the evaluation of the gains and losses from intervention. While specific-factor owners gain from an increase in their industry's domestic relative price, the gains attributable to intervention—and hence the gains pertinent for expression of political support—are given by the increase in factor incomes over and above the income that would have been attained in a free-trade equilibrium in the absence of protection. Similarly, those losing from an increase in the domestic price of the import-competing industry's output express dissatisfaction with policymakers to the extent that an increase in price is due to protection; but domestic policymakers are not held accountable for changes in the exogenous world price of imports. The industry political-support function which policymakers seek to maximize encompasses free trade as the non-intervention reference point and is given by

$$\tilde{M}(P, P^*) = M[\pi(P, P^*), P - P^*] = M[\pi(P) - \pi(P^*), P - P^*]$$

$$(2.1)$$

where P^* is the relative world price of the protected industry's output.

The first argument in (2.1) is the increase in industry-specific rents due to the departure from free trade when protection maintains the domestic price at $P(>P^*)$; the second argument reflects the increase in domestic price over the world price as the source of political dissatisfaction with protection. Political-support responses imply $M_1 > 0$ and $M_2 < 0$. Diminishing marginal political support from increases in protection implies $M_{11} < 0$, and increasing antagonism on the part of losers from protection implies $M_{22} < 0$. An envy effect can be expressed via M_{12}: if losers' antagonism increases, the greater the increases in real income which the gainers from protection are observed to have achieved, then $\partial |M_2|/\partial \pi > 0$, or $M_{12} < 0$. Symmetry implies that M_1 is greater, the more successful the potential losers from protection have been in influencing politically determined trade policy.

The policymaker endogenously determines the industry's level of protection by choosing trade policy to maximize political support given by (2.1). The equilibrium condition for policy choice, as in the industry regulation model, specifies domestic relative price as the outcome of a balancing of political support, here from the gainers and losers from protection:

$$\tilde{M}_p = M_1\pi_p + M_2 = 0 \tag{2.2}$$

or

$$\pi_p = -M_1/M_2. \tag{2.2'}$$

This equilibrium is depicted in Figure 2.1 as yielding a domestic (relative) price $\tilde{P}$.

Let the government implement its protectionist policy via a specific tariff. The domestic price derived from (2.2) is then $P = (P^* + T)$, where T is the political-support maximizing tariff.

Suppose now, reflecting a shift in international comparative advantage, that the exogenous world price P^* of the domestic industry's output were to decrease. If the level of the tariff were independent of political-support considerations, the domestic price P would fall in line with the fall in the world price P^*, and the domestic industry's output would decline as the industry moved down its supply function. However, P^* appears as a parameter in the political-support equilibrium condition (2.2), and hence whether

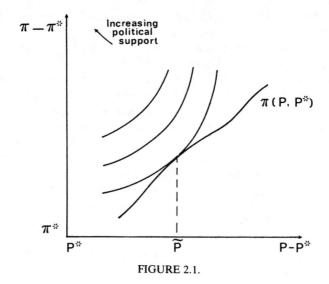

FIGURE 2.1.

the domestic industry will have contracted subsequent to the fall in the world price depends upon the endogenous policy response to the decline in the world price. The industry would not contract at all if the decline in the world price were to be fully offset by a compensatory increase in the tariff.

The policy response to a change in the world price is derived from (2.2) as

$$dP/dP^* = -\tilde{M}_{pp^*}/\tilde{M}_{pp}, \qquad (2.3)$$

where

$$\tilde{M}_{pp^*} = -(M_{11}\pi_p\pi_{p^*} + \pi_p M_{12} + \pi_{p^*}M_{12} + M_{22}) > 0$$
$$\phantom{\tilde{M}_{pp^*} =} {\scriptstyle (-)\ (+)(+)\quad (+)(-)\quad (+)(-)\quad (-)}$$

$$\tilde{M}_{pp} = M_1\pi_{pp} + M_{11}\pi_p^2 + 2\pi_p M_{12} + M_{22} < 0.$$
$$\phantom{\tilde{M}_{pp} =} {\scriptstyle (+)(-)\quad (-)(+)\quad (+)(-)\quad (-)}$$

Since $\tilde{M}_{pp} < 0$ (which confirms the necessary condition for political-support maximization), and $\tilde{M}_{pp^*} > 0$, world and domestic prices move in the same direction when protectionist decisions are based on motives of political support. Hence a decline in the world price of an industry's output results in a decline in the political-support maximizing domestic price.

However, although the domestic price necessarily declines with a fall in the world price, the level of protection may increase or decrease. Since

$$dT/dP^* = dP/dP^* - 1, \qquad (2.4)$$

it follows that

$$dT/dP^* \gtreqless 0 \quad \text{as} \quad dP/dP^* \gtreqless 1 \qquad (2.5)$$

and hence in principle the change in the domestic price may be greater or less than the change in the world price.

Industry decline may therefore be retarded by the government's endogenous policy response, in which case the political-support maximization model of protection is consistent with a shift of comparative advantage away from an industry (P^* falling), declining industry output and decreasing factor-specific rents (P falling), but *increasing* protection in the course of industry decline (T increasing). An increase in protection however never fully compensates factors specific to the import-competing industry for the income loss due to the decline in the world price of the industry's output. Thus as the world price falls the declining industry continues to decline, although the level of the protective tariff may increase or decrease. No incentive is provided by the political protectionist response for entry to occur to dissipate the benefits of the protectionist policy. The beneficiaries of protection remain the owners of the industry's established specific factors at the time protection is provided.

The political self-interest model accordingly explains protectionist responses to shifting comparative advantage without recourse to social-welfare concepts or social-insurance motives for intervention. The model reveals that intervention to retard the decline of an import-competing industry is consistent with trade policy which furthers a government's own political self-interest.

2.2. Changing political support and industry decline

Continued industry decline is thus consistent with trade policy formulated to maximize political support. Protectionist policies might retard industry decline, thereby providing more time for owners of industry-specific assets to adjust to adverse trade-related change; but also a political-support maximizing protectionist response may hasten industry decline.

An analysis of the endogenous policy response in the course of adjustment demonstrates that an industry may be led to exhibit a sudden collapse in output when, in the absence of politically endogenous protection, industry decline would proceed smoothly and no collapse would occur. The possibility of sudden collapse is introduced via the feedback from industry decline to erosion of political support. The collapse of output and employment is formally an instance of a mathematical catastrophe. Sharp discontinuous change takes place, even though interaction is between smoothly adjusting variables, capital and labor, which exit the industry as the industry declines. The two factors however exit at a differential pace. Capital exits slowly at a rate bounded by real depreciation of productive capacity, while labor is more adaptable in adjusting to changing rewards in alternative employment. When the level of protection responds to changes in political support in the course of industry decline, the combination of slowly adjusting capital and faster adjusting labor can lead to the "catastrophe" of sudden industry collapse.

To portray such politically endogenous industry collapse, denote by industry 1 the declining industry and let industry 2 represent the rest of the economy which offers mobile factors alternative employment. In a long-run competitive equilibrium, the values of factors' marginal products are equal across alternative uses, and hence $PF_j^1(L_1, K_1) = F_j^2(L - L_1, K - K_1)$, $j = L, K$, where $P = P_1/P_2$ is the relative price of the declining industry's output and (L, K) are the economy's aggregate factor endowments. When P falls, capital leaves the declining industry at a rate determined by differential factor rewards according to

$$\dot{K}_1 = g(r_1 - r_2) \tag{2.6}$$

where $g(0) = 0$, $g'(\cdot) > 0$, $r_i = P_i F_K^i (i = 1, 2)$. The domestic relative price is $P = (P^* + T)$, where P^* is the exogenous world price and T is the level of tariff protection.

With the tariff T given, Figure 2.2 depicts the long-run equilibrium factor allocation (K_1^a, L_1^a) for the relative price P'. In long-run equilibrium $\dot{L}_1 = \dot{K}_1 = 0$. The labor and capital equilibrium loci have respective slopes

$$\left. \frac{dK_1}{dL_1} \right|_{\dot{L}_i=0} = -\left[\frac{PF_{LL}^1 + F_{LL}^2}{PF_{KL}^1 + F_{KL}^2} \right] > 0, \tag{2.7}$$

$$\left. \frac{dK_1}{dL_1} \right|_{\dot{K}_i=0} = -\left[\frac{PF_{KL}^1 + F_{KL}^2}{PF_{KK}^1 + F_{KK}^2} \right] > 0, \tag{2.8}$$

(since $F_L^i, F_K^i > 0$, $F_{LL}^i, F_{KK}^i < 0$, $F_{KL}^i > 0$) and intersect at the point A, which is a stable equilibrium. When P' declines to P'', the labor-equilibrium locus shifts to the left, reflecting reduced industry demand for labor for any industry employment of capital, and the capital-equilibrium locus shifts downward, correspondingly reflecting reduced industry demand for capital for any associated level of employment of labor. Adjustment from the initial equilibrium at A to the new equilibrium associated with the price P'' begins with labor employment in the industry instantaneously contracting from L_1^a to L_1^b at the preexisting former equilibrium industry capital stock K_1^a. Then, labor adjusts along the labor-equilibrium locus as fast as

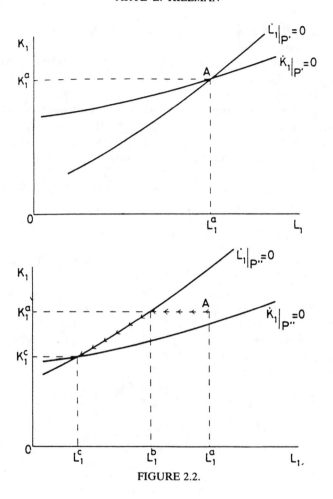

FIGURE 2.2.

K_1 declines via (2.6), until the long-run equilibrium consistent with the price P'' is reached at (K_1^c, L_1^c).

The instantaneous decline in labor employment from L_1^a to L_1^b is not here the characterization of industry collapse. This fall in employment of labor reflects the price decline from P'' to P''', and follows from viewing the fall in the price of output as a once-and-for-all discrete change rather than introducing a dynamic continuous equation for the change in price $\dot{P}$.

The smooth industry adjustment in response to the adverse shift in comparative advantage presumes a passive policy response. Now, however, introduce endogenous politically-motivated protection. Empirical evidence, to be subsequently reviewed, suggests that, other things equal, the level of protection an industry can expect to receive is greater, the greater the number of jobs provided by the protected industry. Thus $T = T(L_1)$, with $T_L > 0$. Labor, although mobile, can be viewed as earning inframarginal rents, and supports (and is appreciative of) protection for the industry wherein it is employed. Higher employment translates into a higher equilibrium level of protection because of political sensitivity to a larger number of beneficiaries from protection. Owners of industry-specific physical capital of course have an interest in supporting protection for the declining industry to which their capital is committed. But stock markets may allow diversification of physical capital portfolios. Here the focus is on the political motive to protect jobs.

Increases in industry size as measured by L_1 may not affect the equilibrium level of protection uniformly. The theory of political coalitions suggests an optimal size for political effectiveness. Too small a coalition may be ineffective in soliciting support in the political arena since the small coalition may have little to offer to offset the political cost of alienating the losers from protection. On the other hand, a coalition may be too large as well for political effectiveness. The relation for $T(L_1)$ as set out in Figure 2.3 implies an optimum size for political effectiveness. At the point of inflection at L_1', the marginal political tariff response is maximal.

The long-run factor-market equilibrium conditions now encompass endogenous protection. Equality of values of marginal product is given by $[P^* + T(L_1)]F_j^1(L_1, K_1) = F_j^2(L - L_1, K - K_1)$, $j = K, L$, giving rise to long-run equilibrium factor-employment loci with the respective slopes

$$\frac{dK_1}{dL_1}\bigg|_{\dot{L}=0} = -\left[\frac{(P^* + T)F_{LL}^1 + F_L^1 T_L + F_{LL}^2}{(P^* + T)F_{KL}^1 + F_{KL}^2}\right] \gtreqless 0; \quad (2.9)$$

$$\frac{dK_1}{dL_1}\bigg|_{\dot{K}=0} = -\left[\frac{(P^* + T)F_{KL}^1 + F_K^1 T_L + F_{KL}^2}{(P^* + T)F_{KK}^1 + F_{KK}^2}\right] > 0. \quad (2.10)$$

The capital-equilibrium locus thus retains its positive slope, but the

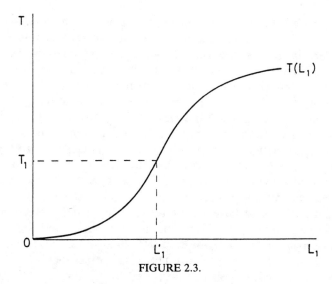

FIGURE 2.3.

labor equilibrium locus can have a range with negative slope, in the manner depicted in Figure 2.4.

With the industry (and the economy) in the stable equilibrium at A, consider again the consequences of a discrete fall in the world price of the industry's output. The politically optimal protectionist

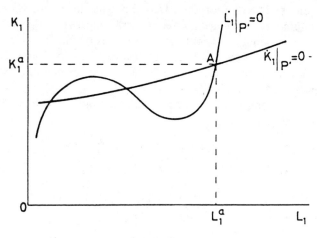

FIGURE 2.4.

response provides less than a full offset for the fall in the world price. Thus, the industry may receive a compensatory increase in protection, but in the political equilibrium the losers from protection (who are the gainers from the initial uncompensated fall in the world price) also are left with some benefit via the policy response. Hence, when the world price declines, the endogenous political-support maximizing policy response is also to permit the domestic price to decline from P' to P''. As depicted in Figure 2.5, the adjustment from the initial equilibrium at A again begins with a decline in labor employment, from L_1^a to L_1^b at the maintained prior equilibrium capital employment K_1^a. Then labor proceeds to exit the declining industry along the labor-equilibrium locus at a rate determined by the exit of capital from the industry, until capital has declined to K_1^c at which the associated labor employment is L_1^c. As employment declines, so does the industry's marginal political effectiveness. At L_1^c the political feedback from industry decline to level of protection leads protection to drop off to such an extent that equality of the value of the marginal product of labor in the declining industry and alternative employment requires an increase in K_1. But there is no incentive for capital to enter the declining industry. Hence the "catastrophe" of sudden discontinuous decline in labor employment, from L_1^c to L_1^d. Then from (K_1^c, L_1^d) industry

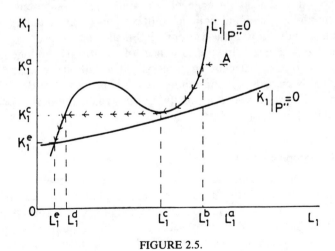

FIGURE 2.5.

decline proceeds smoothly and continuously until the long-run equilibrium consistent with the new industry level of political effectiveness and new equilibrium price of output is attained at (K_1^e, L_1^e).

The collapse occurs because in the course of adjustment fewer and fewer individuals remain to have their jobs (and their infra-marginal rents) protected by the political policy response. One might expect industrial decline initiated by an adverse shift in comparative advantage to be exacerbated by a feedback from loss of political support in the course of decline. While the feedback effect may be expected, the surprise is the sudden abrupt collapse which can occur in the course of industry decline.

A number of industries in the U.S.—shoes, toys, matches, motorcycles, steel, shipbuilding—have experienced the sequence of decline of international competitiveness, a protectionist policy response, further gradual decline in output and protection, and then sharp contraction. The abrupt decline is generally characterized by a sudden exit of the workers with the least to lose, those with low seniority and small accumulation of industry-specific human capital. As the more mobile factors exit, so the returns to the slower adjusting inputs decrease markedly. Workers who do not exit take pay cuts. Physical plant and equipment are suddenly written down in value. When the sudden contraction ceases, the industry settles down to a new sharply lower level of output and employment. The above model of changing political support and industry collapse is consistent with these observations. Political-support protectionist motives are central. In the absence of politically endogenous protection, industry decline in response to a shift in comparative advantage is smooth and continuous. The phenomenon of declining industry collapse arises as a possibility only when political-support protectionist motives are introduced.

2.3. Bibliographic notes

The characterization of the optimizing behavior of governments as making regulatory decisions to maximize a political-support function derives from Stigler (1971) and Peltzman (1976). The adaptation to an international trade setting to explain political-support maximizing protectionist responses for declining industries is based on Hillman (1982). The analysis of changing political support in the course of industry decline and sudden industry collapse is based on Cassing and Hillman (1986).

3. PROTECTION UNDER DIRECT DEMOCRACY

The political self-interest model of protection formulated in the previous section focuses on incumbent governments and stresses the policy discretion attendant on incumbency. The model thus offers predictions concerning how an incumbent government might exercise policy discretion. However, although implicit via the political-support motive, the model does not capture the characteristic that policy or policy discretion may be politically contestable. Contestability may occur in the institutional context of direct democracy or representative democracy; under direct democracy, individuals vote directly on an issue, under representative democracy they vote for representatives to whom responsibility is delegated for direct voting on issues. More usually, protectionist decisions are made in the context of representative democracy. A model of endogenous choice of protection under direct democracy is however instructive in indicating the types of outcomes that might arise were the gainers and losers from protection directly able to participate in the determination of trade policy.

To formulate such a model, suppose that individuals have diverse claims to an economy's factor endowments and that there exist no markets allowing individuals to diversify their factor-ownership portfolios. Each factor owner then has an optimal trade policy which is individually welfare-maximizing; only those individuals who hold claims over factors in proportions duplicating the relative factor endowment of the economy have an interest in supporting a policy of free trade. With majority voting and no voting costs, a country's trade policy is determined by the welfare-maximizing policy of the median voter, and hence by the relation between the median voter's claims over factors and the aggregate endowment. Since the median voter will not in general have claims to factor ownership in the same proportion as the country's relative factor endowments, there is no reason to expect a free-trade outcome.

3.1. The Heckscher–Ohlin case

In the Heckscher–Ohlin case, the economy is endowed with given quantities of intersectorally mobile labor and capital. Individual i has a claim to one unit of labor ($L^i = 1$) and $K^i (\geq 0)$ units of capital. All individuals have identical homothetic preferences in consumption; hence aggregate consumption is independent of the domestic distribution of income derived from diverse factor ownership. The economy confronts given world prices. Revenue from trade taxes is distributed domestically in a lump-sum manner. Revenue distribution is neutral; the share of revenue received by an individual equals his share of factor income. Individual i has an indirect utility function,

$$U^i = U^i(p^*, y^i) = U^i(p, \phi^i Y) \tag{3.1}$$

where $p \equiv p_1/p_2$, y^i is the ith individual's income inclusive of transfer of revenue, Y is the economy's aggregate income, and ϕ^i is the ith individual's income share ($\sum \phi^i = 1$). An ad-valorem tariff t is the instrument of trade policy. Denoting the international terms of trade by p^*, (3.1) can be expressed as a function of the tariff as

$$U^i = U^i(p^*(1+t), \phi^i Y). \tag{3.1'}$$

Individual i's choice of a personally optimal tariff derives from maximization of (3.1'), via the solution to

$$\frac{\partial U^i}{\partial t} = \frac{\partial U^i}{\partial p}\frac{\partial p}{\partial t} + \frac{\partial U^i}{\partial y^i}\frac{\partial y^i}{\partial t} = 0. \tag{3.2}$$

This condition can be transformed, first by using Roy's identity to establish that

$$\frac{\partial U^i}{\partial p} = -D^i\frac{\partial U^i}{\partial y^i} = -\phi^i D\frac{\partial U}{\partial y^i} \tag{3.3}$$

where D^i and D respectively denote consumption of good 1 by the ith individual and aggregate consumption that good. Substituting (3.3) into (3.2) yields

$$\frac{\partial U^i}{\partial t} = \frac{\partial U^i}{\partial y^i}\left\{ -\phi^i D p^* + Y\frac{\partial \phi^i}{\partial t} + \phi^i\frac{\partial Y}{\partial t} \right\} = 0. \tag{3.2'}$$

The expression (3.2') can be simplified by appropriate substitution for $\partial Y/\partial t$. Aggregate income consists of the value of output of the goods X_i $(i = 1, 2)$ produced domestically and tariff revenue; denoting imports (of good 1) by M,

$$Y = pX_1 + X_2 + tp^*M. \tag{3.4}$$

Hence

$$\begin{aligned}\frac{\partial Y}{\partial t} &= p\frac{\partial X_1}{\partial t} + \frac{\partial X_2}{\partial t} + p^*X_1 + tp^*\frac{\partial M}{\partial t} + p^*M\\ &= p^*(X_1 + M) + tp^* \cdot \partial M/\partial t\\ &= D_1 p^* + tp^* \cdot \partial M/\partial t.\end{aligned} \tag{3.5}$$

Substituting (3.5) into (3.2') then yields

$$\frac{\partial U^i}{\partial t} = \frac{\partial U^i}{\partial y^i}\left\{\phi^i tp^*\frac{\partial M}{\partial t} + Y \cdot \frac{\partial \phi^i}{\partial t}\right\} = 0. \tag{3.2''}$$

The optimal tariff of individual i is therefore determined from

$$Y \cdot \frac{\partial \phi^i}{\partial t} = -\phi^i tp^* \frac{\partial M}{\partial t}. \tag{3.6}$$

The LHS of (3.6) reveals the effect of a marginal tariff increase on individual i's welfare via the change in his income share; the RHS expresses the effect on welfare via the change in imports. Since $\partial M/\partial t < 0$, it follows that in the neighborhood of individual i's optimal tariff a marginal tariff increase necessarily increases the income share ϕ^i.

Assuming that $U^i(t)$ is strictly concave, (1.6) can be solved for individual i's unique optimal tariff,

$$\tilde{t}^i = -\left(\frac{Y}{p^* \cdot \partial M/\partial t}\right)\left(\frac{\partial \phi^i}{\partial t} \cdot \frac{1}{\phi^i}\right). \tag{3.6'}$$

Hence,

$$\mathrm{sign}\, t^i = \mathrm{sign}\left(\frac{\partial \phi^i}{\partial t}\right). \tag{3.6''}$$

However,

$$\frac{\partial \phi^i}{\partial t} = \left\{\frac{wL}{(wL + rK)^2(1 + t)}\right\}\left\{\frac{r(k - k^i)(\hat{w} - \hat{r})}{\hat{p}}\right\}, \tag{3.7}$$

where k is the economy's relative factor endowment and k^i is the relative claim over factors of individual i. Via the Stolper–Samuelson Theorem, $(\hat{w} - \hat{r})/\hat{p}$ is respectively positive or negative as imports are respectively relatively labor or capital intensive.

If for example imports are relatively labor intensive,

$$\text{sign}\left(\frac{\partial \phi^i}{\partial t}\right) = \text{sign}(k - k^i). \tag{3.8}$$

Hence (i) $t^i > 0$ if $k > k^i$; that is, an individual benefits from protection if he is relatively less well endowed with capital than the economy as a whole; (ii) the greater is the deviation of individual i's endowment from that of the economy, the greater is that individual's optimal departure from free trade, and (iii) $t^i = 0$ only if $k = k^i$.

Now, let individuals be given the opportunity to vote on tariff levels. In seeking to maximize utility $U^i(p, y^i)$, all individuals confront the same relative price p; so consider the effect of a change in the tariff on the individual's real income y^i. Define the marginal benefit from an increase in the tariff as

$$\frac{\Delta y^i}{\Delta t} = B^i(k^i, t) = \frac{\partial U^i/\partial t}{\partial U^i/\partial y^i}. \tag{3.9}$$

The function B^i has the properties

$$\frac{\partial B^i}{\partial k^i} \gtreqless 0 \quad \text{as imports are} \quad \begin{cases} K \\ L \end{cases} \text{intensive}, \tag{3.10}$$

and

$$\frac{\partial B^i}{\partial t} < 0. \tag{3.11}$$

The property (3.10) follows from the Stolper–Samuelson Theorem. For example, let imports be relatively capital-intensive: then (3.10) indicates that individual i's marginal benefit from a tariff increase is greater, the greater his own individual claim to capital relative to labor. (3.11) follows from the strict concavity of $U(t)$ and the linear homogeneity of degree one of utility in goods consumed.

Figure 3.1 depicts the case where imports are relatively capital intensive (hence $\partial B^i/\partial k^i > 0$). $B_0 B_0$ is the schedule at free trade. k

is the economy's relative factor endowment, and $B(k, 0) = 0$. That is, for an individual i for whom $k^i = k$, a zero tariff (or free trade) is optimal.

Alternatively, consider an individual j with an endowment $\bar{k}^j$ exceeding the economy's endowment k. As indicated in Figure 3.1, for this individual $B(\bar{k}^j, 0) > 0$; that is, at free trade ($t = 0$), such an individual would vote for a positive tariff.

The schedule B_1B_1 depicts $B(k^i, t_1)$ for a positive tariff t_1. The tariff t_1 is welfare-maximizing for the particular individual j whose endowment is $\bar{k}^j$, reflected in $B(\bar{k}^j, t_1) = 0$. At any tariff less than t_1, $B(\bar{k}^j, t) > 0$, and hence it is in the interest of individual j to vote to raise the tariff; at any tariff beyond t_1, $B(\bar{k}^j, t) < 0$ and it is in individual j's interest to vote to decrease the tariff.

Now distribute individual factor owners in accord with their relative factor endowments along the k^i axis. Given his endowment $\bar{k}^j$, each factor owner has an individually optimal tariff $\bar{t}^j$ beyond which he will not vote for further tariff increases. Hence, as the tariff increases, the number of individuals who benefit from further tariff increases declines. The equilibrium tariff for the economy under majority voting is attained when a majority cannot be found to increase a prevailing tariff.

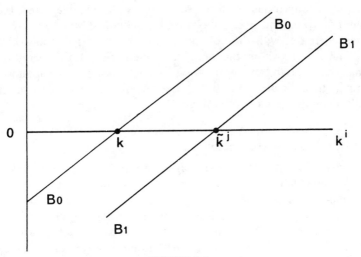

FIGURE 3.1.

Since $U^i(t)$ is strictly concave, individuals' preferences over tariff levels are single-peaked. Hence an equilibrium tariff necessarily exists under majority voting. The equilibrium tariff established for the economy is the individually optimal tariff for the median voter.

The level of the equilibrium tariff therefore depends upon the characteristics of the median voter. In turn, the identity of the median voter depends upon voter eligibility rules and the distribution of factor ownership. Voter eligibility rules which require minimal capitial ownership impart a bias toward protection for the relatively capital-intensive good; on the other hand, the more concentrated is capital ownership, the greater the bias towards protection for the relatively labor-intensive good. Whether a protective tariff will at all arise depends upon the relation between the relative factor claim of the median voter and the economy's aggregate factor endowment. Majority voting will result in a tariff on capital-intensive imports if the median voter is better endowed with capital than the economy as a whole. An outcome of free trade arises only in the special case where, for all individuals who are entitled to (and do) vote, the distribution of factor ownership is such that the median voter's factor endowment happens to correspond to the economy's aggregate endowment.

The cost of voting has been assumed to be zero. However, one may wish to introduce positive voting costs. All eligible voters then may not vote. The probability that an individual will vote suggestively increases with the net gain from voting. In particular, those individuals for whom the marginal benefit of a tariff increase is small have no incentive to vote; potential voter participation is limited to individuals for whom the benefit of an increase in the tariff exceeds the costs of voting.

3.2. The specific-factors case

The cost of voting plays a more significant role when one leaves the Heckscher–Ohlin framework and considers majority voting in a specific-factors setting. Then the benefits from protection are concentrated in a particular industry, but the losses are more diffusely spread throughout the economy. For given costs of voter participation, industry-specific interests benefitting from a tariff have a greater incentive, and are more likely, to vote than the losers from protection. Hence, in a model of direct democracy and majority voting, positive voting costs can explain how a majority of *participating* voters may favor tariff increases for an industry, when a majority of *eligible* voters loses from such protection.

3.3. Bibliographic notes

The model of the determination of protectionist equilibrium under direct democracy set out in this section is based on Wolfgang Mayer (1984).

4. PROTECTION UNDER REPRESENTATIVE DEMOCRACY

4.1. Direct vs. representative democracy

Direct democracy is not commonly the institutional setting wherein trade policy is decided. The more usual political system is that of representative democracy, where trade policy decisions are made by elected representatives. Under representative democracy, individuals do not have the opportunity of using their vote to influence trade policy directly, but they can seek to secure the election of a representative whose views on the issue of protection for a particular industry reflect their own (or, of course, an individual can himself stand for election).

In principle, policy outcomes under direct and representative democracy could coincide. Political competition would result in the duplication under representative democracy of the outcomes under direct democracy, given majority voting. Candidates whose views reflected those of the median voter would win election, while the motive of reelection would keep elected incumbents committed to majority-supported policy positions; and if the preferences of voters were to change to alter the policy supported by the majority, the policy position of winning candidates would likewise change.

In practice, however, disciplining of incumbent representatives by voters may be limited. Incumbents tend to be favored by political entry barriers. As well, voters are in general obliged to vote for candidates on the basis of the stand taken on a bundle of issues, rather than a single issue such as protection for one particular industry. Rational voters will also not have the incentive to acquire information on all policy issues since, independently of the problem of bundling of issues, the probability of being the decisive median voter in any election is small. It may therefore be rational for individual voters to be ignorant about candidates' policy positions. These considerations allow candidates for political office and elected representatives to exercise policy discretion. The consequence is that policy choices under representative democracy need not duplicate the outcomes that would obtain under direct democracy.

How might policy outcomes under direct and representative democracy differ? One possibility is that elected representatives may adopt policy positions on some issues which are consistent with a personal maintained ideology rather than reflecting the preferences of their constituents. But, if not bound by voters' preferences, the behavior of elected representatives need not be explained by adherence to policy positions precommitted by ideology or personal preference. An alternative hypothesis is that the policy positions adopted by candidates for political office and by elected representatives are subject to the influence of special interests. The political support offered by special interests can be directed towards the objective of success in competition for political office.

Voters' preferences may also be manipulable. Campaign expenditures which influence the probability of political success may also affect policy determination via outlays made to change voters' perceptions of the desirability of different policies. Underlying the possibilty of influencing voter's preferences is again rational ignorance: the acquisition or confirmation of information by individual voters is costly while under majority voting the expected benefit derived from application of any information acquired to vote one's self-interest at the polls is small.

Further, since the expected benefit from voting is small, rational individuals whose value of time is positive suggestively have little incentive to participate by voting in political contests. Given that the likelihood of a single vote being decisive in determining an electoral outcome will tend to be small, recourse to other than individual economic benefit-cost calculation may be required to explain voter participation. The disincentive for individuals to vote because of the small likelihood of affecting the outcome is an additional influence increasing the policy discretion of an incumbent politician in a system of representative democracy.

4.2. Coalition formation

The above considerations suggest that under representative democracy the links between the preferences of an individual voter, the exercise of the right to vote, and the determination of policy on a particular issue may be tenuous. However, coalitions of individuals seeking a common objective may be more politically effective. The coalition may offer a block of organized votes, or sizeable campaign contributions. Either way, the attainment of critical mass via coalition formation may provide the political effectiveness that individuals left to themselves may not be able to achieve. In the context of a study of the determination of protection, the pertinent coalitions are composed of the gainers and losers from protection.

The gainers and losers tend to be asymmetric in numbers. The industry-specific interests who gain from protection of a particular industry tend to be smaller in number than the losers in the rest of the economy. While this may be an evident disadvantage if trade policy is decided by a direct vote under direct democracy, it may on the contrary be an advantage in a system of representative democracy. Political activity directed at securing protection is in the nature of a public good. The owner of an industry-specific factor who succeeds in evoking a protectionist response benefits all other owners of factors specific to the same industry. Likewise, an individual who loses from protection and succeeds in preempting or moderating a protectionist response benefits all other like individuals in the economy. The theory of collective action to influence trade policy thus becomes intertwined with the theory of collective provision of public goods.

For any coalition contributing towards a collective objective yielding a public-good benefit, the collectively efficient aggregate contribution satisfies the condition, well-known in the public-finance literature (and associated with Paul Samuelson) that the sum of individual marginal benefits equal marginal costs. For a coalition of gainers from protection, this condition establishes the collectively rational level of political activity directed at seeking to influence trade policy. However, it is individually rational for each beneficiary of protection to defect from the collectively rational contribution assigned the individual—given that the attempt at coordinated political activity is not to be repeated. The conflict between collectively and individually rational behavior that confronts beneficiaries of (and losers from) protection is indicative of a Prisoners' Dilemma. If individuals act independently, and optimize on the assumption that their actions do not affect the actions of others, the level of political activity undertaken by individuals will be that given by a Nash equilibrium. The Nash level of political activity will be less than that which is collectively optimal, a reflection of free-riding rather than cooperative behavior.

Nevertheless, all other things equal, in general when individuals act noncooperatively in deciding on their contributions towards a public good, a larger coalition will contribute more than a smaller coalition. Hence, with independent Nash behavior, increased size remains an advantage. The overall level of political activity by a larger group will exceed that of a smaller group. Suggestively, the more numerous losers from protection have an advantage over the smaller number of gainers.

However, all other things are not equal. A distinguishing asymmetry is the value of the political prize as perceived by gainers and losers from protection. The gainers from protection are seeking to influence policy which bears directly on their incomes derived from ownership of industry-specific factors of protection. In an economy with many industries, the income transfer to the gainers from protection of one industry is spread over many losers from protection (who also bear the deadweight loss). Viewed in terms of the interests of producers and consumers, producers may seek via influence over trade policy to increase their rents, whereas individual consumers in general spend but a small portion of their incomes on a particular protected good. The stakes in political contests therefore differ for individual members of the gaining and losing coalitions from protection.

If the coalition of gainers is sufficiently small, the gainers may be able to effect a cooperative rather than noncooperative outcome. With small numbers, individual behavior is more readily monitorable, and defection from cooperative behavior may therefore be more readily observable. Further, if the need to cooperate is perceived to be recurring indefinitely as one might expect to be the case with the quest to maintain an influence over policy over time, the individually rational response may be cooperative behavior rather than defection. An individual strategy of "tit for tat" (rewarding cooperation by cooperating and punishing defecting by defecting) may lead all agents acting independently without coordination to adopt the collectively rational response. However, the very large numbers of the losers from protection may persist in their individually rational (but collectively suboptimal) contributions to the common objective of preempting or moderating protection for an industry.

Small numbers may also be conducive to what has been described as matching behavior; that is, behavior whereby individuals match each others' contributions at preannounced matching rates to yield the cooperative collectively rational equilibrium level of outlays on a public good.

Size is beneficial under direct democracy where votes count. However, under representative democracy, given asymmetries in the distribution of benefits and costs of particular protectionist policies, it would appear that size may be a hindrance. Certainly, the evidence is that a coalition bound together by a common industry-specific income source can be effective in securing income transfers via protection at the expense of larger coalitions of losers from protectionist policies. The "cohesive" gainers from protection tend to fare better under representative democracy than the more "diffuse" losers.

4.3. Lobbying equilibria

Suppose now that coalitions of gainers and losers from protection seek to influence trade policy by lobbying. Protection endogenously determined by lobbying activities of self-interested coalitions has been investigated in the setting of both the specific-factors and Hecksher–Ohlin models of international trade. The typical procedure is to introduce a tariff-formation function. For example, in a specific-factors setting Findlay and Wellisz (1982) portray the political tariff-setting mechanism via a function $t = t(L_1, L_2)$ indicating the height of the tariff t provided to the import-competing industry 1 when allocations of mobile labor, L_1 and L_2, are chosen as Nash-equilibrium lobbying inputs by the two opposing specific-factor coalitions. The coalitions themselves are not subject to disincentives associated with the public-good nature of the political activity that they undertake. Lobbying by any one coalition is assumed to be subject to diminishing returns. Tariff revenue is redistributed in lump-sum fashion to consumers. Thus, lump-sum redistribution of income via tariff-revenue transfers is possible. However, the coalitions are obliged to use labor services to effect (or prevent) income transfers via protection.

Equilibrium in models based on such tariff-formation functions need not be unique. There may for example be two Nash equilibria for lobbying by the two coalitions, one with a higher level of protection but with fewer resources having been used in lobbying activities, and the other equilibrium exhibiting a lower level of protection but with more resources having been used in lobbying by the two coalitions. The cost of the tariff here consists of the production and consumption inefficiency losses due to protection, plus the opportunity cost of using productive labor in lobbying activities. It is therefore not possible to specify in general in which of such two equilibria the total cost of protection will be lower. The higher tariff results in higher efficiency losses, but fewer productive resources may have been used in the activity of seeking to influence trade policy. Consequently, in the presence of lobbying, higher observed tariff levels do not necessarily imply a higher cost of protection. A free-trade equilibrium may for example only be sustained via the successful lobbying of free-trade interests who have allocated substantial resources to counter the resources allocated to lobbying by protectionist interests.

In an alternative lobbying formulation using a similar tariff-formation function in a Heckscher–Ohlin setting, Feenstra and Bhagwati (1982) model a contest not between the gainers and losers from protection, but between a government and one of the two coalitions of factors owners, the other coalition remaining passive.

The government does not have a political-support maximizing objective. The objective is to maximize social welfare.

Lobbying by an interest group is triggered by a change in the relative world price of output. For example, if the domestic import-competing sector is relatively labor-intensive and the terms of trade improve, labor seeks to recoup some of its Stolper–Samuelson based losses by lobbying for a tariff. The government is responsive to lobbying only by the group which has suffered a fall in income because of the change in the terms of trade. Owners of capital, who will have gained from the change in the economy's terms of trade, therefore in this model do not expend resources in lobbying. Capital and labor can both be employed in lobbying activity. The tariff formation function is $t = t(L_i, K_i)$ where labor L_i and capital K_i are the lobbying inputs. The cost function for lobbying activities is assumed to take the form

$$C(t, w, r) = \left\{ \frac{t\phi(w, r)}{\max\{0, p_0^* - p^*(1 + t)\}} \right\} \tag{4.1}$$

where $\phi(w, r)$ is an increasing, quasi-concave function, w and r are competitive market prices paid for labor and capital inputs used in lobbying, p_0^* is the relative world price of the import-competing industry's output which prevailed before the change in the terms of trade, and p^* is the new prevailing world price. (4.1) implies that sufficient protection is never forthcoming to return the domestic price of the labor-intensive good to its initial value: costs of lobbying approach infinity as the tariff-inclusive domestic price $p^*(1 + t)$ approaches its original level p_0^*. This formulation of government response to lobbying is thus consistent with the portrayal of policymakers' behavior in terms of maximization of political support in Section 2; in response to an exogenous change which makes ones group worse off, the government effects a change in income distribution via trade policy such that the losing group is compensated, but only partially.

The protectionist coalition chooses an allocation of factors K_i and L_i to lobbying, so as to maximize its collective indirect utility,

$$V(p, I) = V[p^*(1 + t), w\bar{L} - C(t, w, r)]. \tag{4.2}$$

Denoting by x the coalition's per capita consumption of the protected good (which is assumed relatively labor-intensive), the equilibrium condition describing the tariff achieved via lobbying is

$$p^* \left[\bar{L} \frac{dw}{dp} - x \right] = \frac{dC}{dt}. \tag{4.3}$$

The LHS of (4.3) expresses the marginal benefit of lobbying, which is the increase achieved in real income. The RHS is the marginal cost of lobbying, encompassing changing domestic factor prices for the inputs used in lobbying as the tariff changes.

Implicit in this model of endogenous protection is non-monolithic government. For example, the responsiveness of Congress to lobbying might determine lobbying outlays. The executive maximizes social welfare subject to pressure-group lobbying, and thereby in effect optimizes subject to the susceptibility of Congress to influence by lobbying.

4.4. Compensatory transfers and lobbying

A central feature of the Feenstra–Bhagwati model of lobbying is the proposal of a compensation scheme whereby tariff revenue would be used to dissipate protectionist pressure. Equation (4.3) establishes the equilibrium tariff achieved by lobbying. Given the responsiveness to lobbying embedded in the cost-of-lobbying function, the government chooses a level of protection. Since the government is guided by an objective of maximizing social welfare, it seeks to minimize the efficiency costs of departure from free trade. Feenstra and Bhagwati propose that, rather than redistributing the revenue in a neutral manner (if possible), the government give the tariff revenue to the protection-seeking coalition. They suggest that the revenue can thereby be used to persuade the protectionist coalition to accept a lower level of protection than achieved in the lobbying equilibrium described by (4.3). The protectionist coalition would do as well as it would have done, had the tariff achieved via (4.3) been maintained; but owners of capital gain from the transfer of tariff revenue, since the tariff is lower than it otherwise would have been, and hence, via the Stolper–Samuelson theorem, the real return to capital is higher. The transfer of tariff revenue is thus Pareto improving, and hence the tariff is "efficient."

Such transfer of tariff revenue is ostensibly unanticipated. Otherwise, anticipation of direct compensation for gains achieved by lobbying for a protective tariff could increase the expected reward to pressure groups from lobbying activity. Thus, suppose that the protectionist coalition engages in lobbying activities with an awareness that government policy will consist of a protection plus compensation response. That is, the protectionist coalition internalizes the government's tariff-revenue transfer. With the coalition aware that it is to be the beneficiary of the revenue derived from the tariff for which it is lobbying, the LHS of (4.2) includes a further term reflecting the marginal change in the protectionist coalition's real income due to the transfer of tariff revenue. Since there is now an additional potential benefit from lobbying (via the revenue transfer), the transfer of tariff revenue rather than dissipating protectionist pressure could well increase protectionist pressure, by increasing the perceived gain from protection. Whether the equilibrium tariff is reduced or increased depends upon the value of the maximum-revenue tariff. Once the maximum-revenue tariff is reached, the protectionist coalition is inhibited in lobbying for further tariff increases by the declines that it knows will follow in the value of tariff revenue transferred.

4.5. Political competition

The above models do not portray the political competition underlying representative democracy. Lobbying outlays are made, but candidates for political office have no active role in announcing policies in response to the lobbying of special interests. Young and Magee (1986) present a model with simultaneous strategic behavior by two contending coalitions of factor owners and also political competition between two rival parties contending for political office. A Heckscher–Ohlin setting is assumed. Each political party preassociates itself with the interests of one of the factors and proposes policy intervention which benefits the factor owners to whose interests it is committed. The parties' special-interest policy positions are constrained by general voter dissatisfaction with the dispensing of political favors. Factor owners influence the probability of their party's success at the polls by direct contributions of factors of production to the political party of their choice. Mobile labor contributes labor to the pro-labor party, mobile capital contributes capital to the pro-capital party. Lobbying contributions maximize factor owners' expected utilities. Parties' policy positions and factor owners' contributions are chosen with each party acting as a Stackelberg leader with respect to its associated special-interest factor coalition but otherwise all parties and coalitions adopt Nash behavior with respect to one another. Using Cobb–Douglas specifications for goods' unit-cost functions and individuals' utility functions, and a logit model to specifiy a party's probability of electoral success, Young and Magee characterize the equilibrium, which consists of a set of mutually consistent actions whereby the parties designate the extent to which they are prepared to adopt special-interest policies if elected, and the special-interest coalitions specify the lobbying contributions which they are prepared to make to influence the electoral outcome. A unique interior equilibrium is shown to exist, provided that the economy's relative factor endowment satisfies a certain boundedness condition.

Since capital owners allocate some of their capital to contributions which increase the probability of the pro-capital party's success, an increase in an economy's endowment of capital changes equilibrium policies and equilibrium contributions so as to increase capital-owners' expected utilities; and similarly for labor. Hence, whereas the factor-price equalization theorem would predict that within the cone of diversification changes in an economy's relative factor endowment would leave factor rewards unchanged (but via the Rybczynski theorem alter the economy's output mix), the Young–Magee model of political competition superimposed on Heckscher–Ohlin predicts an expected gain for the factor whose domestic supply has increased. This reflects a wealth effect. Increased wealth translates directly into increased political power and into an increased likelihood of success at the polls. Since real resources are used in influencing the probabilities of electoral success, it is further possible for all factor owners to have lost in the endogenous policy equilibrium relative to a free-trade equilibrium wherein political parties are absent and no political contributions are made.

4.6. Bibliographic notes

On collective choice and coalition formation under representative democracy, see Mancur Olson (1966), Peter Bernholz (1966, 1974). Chamberlin (1974) reexamines some of Olson's propositions. See also McGuire (1974). The pioneering paper on the endogeneity of protection and the real-resource cost of politically contestable trade policy is by Tullock (1967). Baldwin (1976) compares direct and representative democracy outcomes. The relation between representatives' ideology and constituents' interests has been studied by Kau and Rubin (1979), Peltzman (1984), and Kalt and Zupan (1984, 1988). Panda (1975) has investigated the relation between campaign expenditures and electoral success. Brock and Magee (1978, 1980) investigate the lobbying behavior of coalitions under representative democracy and provide foundations for the later analyses in Findlay and Wellisz (1982), Feenstra and Bhagwati (1982) and Young and Magee (1986). Young (1982) provides a reformulation of the Findlay–Wellisz (1982) model demonstrating the non-uniqueness of Nash equilibrium. On independent behavior which can lead to a cooperative outcome, see Guttman (1978), Hirschleifer (1982), Axelrod (1984). Guttman (1985) examines U.S. evidence on campaign contributions and suggests that "matching behavior" may better explain the data that noncooperative Nash behavior. For another proposal for a compensatory transfer scheme, see Hufbauer and Rosen (1986). McKenzie (1986) notes the disincentive effects of compensatory transfer schemes. On incentives to lobby and revenue transfers, see Hillman (1988).

5. SHADOW PRICES OF FACTORS AND THE SOCIAL COST OF LOBBYING

5.1. Contesting trade policy

One might suppose that, since lobbying to influence trade policy is an activity using real resources in attempts to effect income transfers, lobbying activity necessarily gives rise to a social loss. Thus Gordon Tullock (1967) proposed that:

These expenditures, which may simply offset each other to some extent, are purely wasteful from the standpoint of society as a whole; they are spent not in increasing wealth, but in attempting to transfer or resist transfer of wealth.

Tullock's position is one that has much intuitive appeal. After all, presumably the time, effort and resources which go into lobbying for protection have more productive alternative uses.

However, Jagdish Bhagwati (1980) has pointed out that one cannot rule out the possibility that the use of resources in lobbying to influence trade policy may actually be socially beneficial. Bhagwati's proposition, which on first reflection may appear somewhat counterintuitive, follows directly as an implication of another theory associated with Bhagwati, that of immiserizing growth. Since it is possible for a small trading economy in a protected equilibrium to lose in aggregate from increased availability of a factor of production, an economy can conversely gain if the same factor is withdrawn from domestic production and is used instead in an unproductive activity such as lobbying. Bhagwati (1982) therefore characterizes lobbying activities as "directly" wasteful but as potentially indirectly productive.

This distinction has implications for the social cost of protection in the previously considered lobbying models. If in a specific-factors setting the contending parties are viewed as allocating mobile labor to lobbying activities, lobbying and counterlobbying are necessarily socially wasteful activities, since the shadow price of mobile labor in a specific-factors model is necessarily positive. However, in a Heckscher–Ohlin setting, one of the mobile factors used in lobbying activity may have a negative shadow price in a protected equilibrium. Feenstra and Bhagwati (1982) accordingly make explicit allowance for negative shadow prices and distinguish between situations where lobbying is socially wasteful and beneficial. Some counterintuitive implications emerge. If the shadow price of the factors used in lobbying is negative, the government's social-welfare maximizing compensation policy is to use the transfer of tariff revenue to induce the protectionist coalition to increase its lobbying activity. By increasing its lobbying efforts, the coalition withdraws additional resources with negative shadow prices from domestic production, hence giving rise to a welfare gain. Another perhaps counterintuitive aspect of this approach to lobbying activity is that lobbying which is at the margin welfare-improving requires a protectionist coalition to have been successful in evoking a protectionist response from government. Unsuccessful lobbying, or lobbying and countervailing lobbying which sustains a free-trade equilibrium, can only be welfare-reducing; for in the neighborhood of free trade, with no distortionary tariff present, shadow prices of the economy's factors of production are necessarily positive.

5.2. Contesting rents and revenues

Lobbying may not only be directed at influencing trade policy, but also at securing rents or revenues associated with trade restrictions. Thus, Anne Krueger (1974) observed that when rights to an import quota are contestable, individuals confront incentives to allocate resources to seeking to become the beneficiaries of the quota rents. Krueger proposed that the resources allocated to the quest for quota rents should therefore be included as a component of the cost of protection in addition to resource-misallocation and consumption inefficiency costs.

Krueger's observation regarding the contestability of quota rents introduced an asymmetry between quota and tariff protection. Quota protection was suggestively more costly because the resources used in seeking quota rents had no counterpart in the case of a tariff.

Bhagwati and Srinivasan (1980) have however proposed that a tariff counterpart of the seeking of quota rents does exist: they have suggested that just as resources may be allocated to contesting the rights to quota rents, so resources may be used in seeking to influence a government in its transfer of tariff revenue. "Revenue seeking" under a tariff is the proposed counterpart to "rent seeking" under a quota.

5.3. Lobbying and tariff/quota asymmetry

Suppose that tariff revenue and quota rights are both contestable, as Bhagwati and Srinivasan suggest. An important asymmetry can nevertheless be identified between competitive tariff and quota equilibria. Consider a competitive economy in a protected equilibrium with no resources directed at contesting the rents or revenues from trade restrictions. The nature of the equilibrium remains independent of whether a tariff or quota is the means of protection (i.e., there is tariff/quota symmetry) so long as no revenue or rent seeking takes place. Allowing for contestability of tariff revenue in a tariff-protected equilibrium and quota premia in a quota-protected equilibrium introduces an asymmetry between the equilibria. Lobbying for tariff revenues (revenue seeking) can possibly be welfare improving. However, lobbying for quota rents (rent seeking) is necessarily a socially costly activity. Or equivalently, in a tariff-protected equilibrium a factor may have a negative shadow price and so withdrawal of that factor from production can be socially beneficial. Shadow prices of factors in a quota-protected equilibrium are however necessarily positive.

This asymmetry arises independently of whether lobbying is directed at influencing trade policy or contesting the rents and revenues due to trade restrictions. The source of the asymmetry has been demonstrated by Anam (1982). Consider a small competitive economy with an aggregate welfare index $U(c_1, c_2)$ where c_i is domestic consumption of good i, and denote the economy's outputs by x_i $(i = 1, 2)$. Let $\bar{K}$ and $\bar{L}$ be the economy's endowments of capital and labor, and assume a Heckscher–Ohlin setting. Shadow prices of labor and capital are respectively defined as $w^* \equiv dU/d\bar{L}$ and $r^* \equiv dU/d\bar{K}$. The possibility of a welfare gain from lobbying activity requires that either w^* or r^* be negative.

Consumers maximize utility, and hence with P_c denoting the domestic relative price confronting consumers, $P_c = U_2/U_1$. Competitive domestic producers confront the relative price P_p. The economy's international trade is balanced, so with P^* denoting the terms of trade,

$$c_1 + P^*c_2 = x_1 + P^*x_2. \tag{5.1}$$

Or, equivalently,

$$c_1 = (x_1 + P_p x_2) + (P^* - P_p)x_2 - P^*c_2. \tag{5.2}$$

The shadow price of labor can be expressed as:

$$\frac{dU}{d\bar{L}} = U_1 \left[\frac{dc_1}{d\bar{L}} + P_c \frac{dc_2}{d\bar{L}} \right]. \tag{5.3}$$

From (5.2),

$$\frac{dc_1}{d\bar{L}} = \frac{dy}{d\bar{L}} + (P^* - P_p)\frac{dx_2}{d\bar{L}} - P^* \frac{dc_2}{d\bar{L}}, \tag{5.4}$$

where $y = (x_1 + P_p x_2)$ is the value of domestic output at the given relative domestic output price. Substituting (5.4) into (5.3) yields the expression for the shadow price of labor,

$$\frac{dU}{d\bar{L}} = U_1 \left[\frac{dy}{d\bar{L}} + (P^* - P_p)\frac{dx_2}{d\bar{L}} + (P_c - P^*)\frac{dc_2}{d\bar{L}} \right]. \tag{5.5}$$

A similar expression obtains for the shadow price of the second factor, capital.

The expression (5.5) can be used to evaluate shadow prices of factors in policy regimes where because of tax-subsidy policies consumer and producer prices differ. With either a tariff or a quota, domestic producer and consumer prices are equal. Hence (5.5) becomes

$$\frac{dU}{d\bar{L}} = U_1\left[\frac{dy}{d\bar{L}} + (P - P^*)\frac{dE_2}{d\bar{L}}\right] \tag{5.6}$$

where $P = P_c = P_p$ is the common price confronting domestic consumers and producers and $E_2 = (c_2 - x_2)$ denotes imports (of good 2).

An increase in the availability of labor increases the value of domestic output at given domestic prices; hence $dy/d\bar{L}$ in (5.6) is positive. Because of protection, $(P - P^*)$ is also positive. A necessary condition for the shadow price of labor to be negative is therefore that $dE_2/d\bar{L}$ be negative; that is, an increase in the availability of labor results in a decline in imports. Immiserization is therefore a possibility if increased availability of a factor leads low opportunity-cost imports to be replaced by high opportunity-cost domestic production.

Now, let the instrument of protection be a tariff, and let labor be the factor exclusively used in lobbying when x_2 is relatively labor-intensive in production. Via the Rybczynski Theorem, allocation of labor to lobbying leads output of x_2 to decline and that of x_1 to expand. If both goods are normal in consumption, imports therefore increase. The converse of immiserization may then occur. Welfare increases if the efficiency gain achieved by replacement of high-cost domestic production by low-cost imports exceeds the loss due to the decrease in the value of output y when employment of labor in domestic production is reduced.

Alternatively, let the means of protection be a quota. Then when labor is withdrawn for use in lobbying activities, imports cannot expand but remain constrained by the binding quota. Hence in (5.6) $dE_2/d\bar{L} = 0$. However, y falls. Therefore, in a quota regime, the withdrawal of a factor from production of goods for use in lobbying necessarily results in an aggregate welfare loss.

Consequently, returning to Krueger's case of rent seeking for quota rights, the resources used in contesting quota premia reflect a social cost of protection, although the same need not be true of resources which have been allocated to the contest to become beneficiaries of a transfer of tariff revenue.

It has moreover been noted by a number of authors that whereas rights to quotas are often contestable, this is rarely the case with respect to rights to tariff revenue, which is in general preallocated to the Treasury. The non-contestability of tariff revenue in practice sustains Krueger's original proposal regarding the higher social cost via rent seeking of quota protection.

5.4. Lobbying by foreigners

Steven Husted (1986) presents evidence of substantial domestic lobbying activity by foreigners in the U.S., including lobbying directed at influencing domestic trade policy. The inputs used in lobbying may be purchased in domestic markets. Whether these inputs have positive or negative shadow prices, foreigners pay— hence lobbying activities even if unproductive are undertaken at foreign expense.

5.5. Bibliographic notes

The observation that the activity of lobbying for protection may be welfare-improving because of negative shadow prices of factors is due to Bhagwati (1980, 1982). The notion of revenue seeking as a quest to become the beneficiary of tariff revenue and the potential of social gain from such activity are due to Bhagwati and Srinivasan (1980, 1982). The resource cost of contesting quota rents was proposed by Krueger (1974), similar arguments having previously made by Tullock (1967, 1971). The demonstration of tariff/quota asymmetry when rents and revenues from trade taxes and quotas are contestable is based on Anam (1982).

6. THE RESOURCE COST OF POLITICAL CONTESTABILITY

We have observed that when protection is endogenously deter-mined via the political process, a cost of protection additional to the consumption inefficiency and resource-misallocation costs is poten-tially introduced, via the value of the real resources used in efforts to influence trade policy. Let us now abstract from the possibility, noted by Bhagwati (1980) and discussed in the previous section, that in protection-distorted equilibria resources may have negative shadow prices. Rather, let us assume that the resources directed at seeking to influence trade policy could be more productively used in activities which *increase* national income, as opposed to attempts to *change* income distribution via protection. If this is so, the use of resources in contests to influence policy outcomes has an associated real cost. This section is concerned with the measurement of this cost.

6.1. The complete dissipation assumption

The procedure in the early analyses which recognized the social cost of political contestability of trade policy was to assume that the value of the prize being contested—the gains from protection or assignment of the rents or revenues from trade intervention— precisely reflected the real value of the resources allocated to influencing the outcome of the political contest. That is, rent dissipation was taken to be complete. This requires that a number of conditions hold. A set of sufficient conditions is that in competitive contests contenders are risk neutral, there are constant returns from outlays made, there is symmetric information, the prize is identically valued by all contenders, no special relationships exist which provide some contenders with advantages over others, and the source of the prize to the winner is not transfers made by the losers. Any one of these conditions may of course fail to hold.

6.2. Risk aversion

Risk-averse behavior might in particular be anticipated to com- promise the presumption of complete rent dissipation, since risk- averse individuals allocate less than the expected benefit from winning a contest to influencing the outcome in their favor. Suppose that all the above conditions for complete rent dissipation are satisfied, other than risk neutrality. Let V denote the common value of the gain to the successful contender in a political contest, let A denote the initial wealth of n identical contenders, and let x indicate the lobbying outlay made by each contender in seeking to influence the policy decision in his favor. Let the lobbying outlay x be chosen to maximize expected utility, and let all individuals have the common utility function $U(\cdot)$. In equilibrium, the expected utility from participation in a political contest to influence policy equals the utility obtainable with certainty via non-participation. Hence in equilibrium

$$EU = [(n-1)/n]U(A-x) + (1/n)U[A-x+V] = U(A). \quad (6.1)$$

By taking a Taylor's expansion and via some further manipulation, one derives the expression for competitive rent dissipation,

$$\lim_{n \to \infty} \frac{nx}{V} = 1 - \frac{kR}{2}, \quad (6.2)$$

where $k \equiv V/A$ and R is relative risk aversion. The total value of outlays made by all contenders is nx, and hence the proportion of the rent dissipated in the political contest is given by nx/V. (6.2) confirms that rent dissipation is complete if contenders are risk neutral ($R = 0$). However, substantial portions of contested rents are dissipated when contenders are risk averse. For example, if $R = 1$ (logarithmic utility) and $k = 0.1$, dissipation is 95 percent; if the value of the rent is increased to 20 percent of initial wealth ($k = 0.2$), 90 percent of the rent is dissipated.

The expression (6.2) is limited in its applicability to small rents (due to the nature of derivation, via a Taylor's expansion). For relatively large rents, establishing the extent of dissipation requires a specification for utility. Simulations using logarithmic utility (so relative risk aversion is unity, as in the examples above) reveal that, for values of rents which are large relative to initial wealth, substantial portions of a rent can be left undissipated.

Hence, for small rents, risk aversion does not substantively compromise the association between the value of a contested rent and resources used in lobbying; but this is not so in cases where the rents contested are large relative to contenders' initial wealth.

The prize V to the winner of the political contest in (6.2) is indivisibly allocated to the winner. However, the prize may well be divisible. For example, the contest may be for a share of the rents associated with assignment of quota rights. There is then uncertainty as to the share of a rent that a contender will obtain rather than uncertainty as to the ultimate recipient of a contested rent. When contenders share the prize sought, the rent-dissipation condition (6.2) generalizes for number of contenders n large to

$$\frac{nC(x)}{V} = 1 - \frac{kR}{2}n\sigma^2 \quad (6.3)$$

where $C(x)$ is the cost of the inputs x used in lobbying, and σ^2 is the variance of the distribution describing the allocation of the rent V among contenders. R is again relative risk aversion and k is the share of the rent relative to initial wealth. Since $n\sigma^2 < 1$, rent dissipation is increased beyond what it would be, were an indivisible rent to be assigned to a successful contender. As in (6.2), rent dissipation is complete if contenders are risk neutral.

6.3. Strategic behavior

Assume now risk neutrality, and let us depart from the assumption that contests to influence policy decisions have sufficiently large numbers of participants to ensure an approximation to competitive behavior. We therefore have small numbers and strategic behavior. Let lobbying outlays be made independently or noncooperatively.

The outcome of small-numbers contests is sensitive to the decision rule for choosing the winner. The rule may be perfectly discriminating, as where the contender making the highest outlay wins the political prize. Or, the rule may be imperfectly discriminating, as where individuals' outlays to influence the outcome of a political contest determine the probability of winning but no actual selection of the winner is made on the basis of ex-ante lobbying allocations.

A further important characteristic of a contest concerns the source of the political prize to the winner. In political contests to influence trade policy, the groups of factor owners who are successful in their quest for protection secure an income transfer at the expense of the losers from protection. The latter not only bear the deadweight losses associated with protectionist policies, but a component of their income decline (exclusive of the deadweight loss) provides the transfer to the gainers from protection. Hence, in a contest to influence policy which redistributes income, contenders seek not only to secure the prize associated with winning, but also seek to avoid bearing the losses associated with losing. Such contests which entail transfers from losers to gainers can be designated transfer contests, as distinct from contests for preexisting rents.

In a contest for a preexisting rent, as in Krueger's contests to become the beneficiary of a quota rent, the prize is not a transfer from the losers in the contest. Since the prize is a prespecified rent, such contests are more properly examples of what has been described as 'rent-seeking' activity.

6.4. A basic model

A basic model will now be formulated portraying the allocation of resources to influence policy in a small-numbers strategic setting. Let n contenders seek to influence policy, and let agent i outlay x_i to influence the outcome of the contest in his favor. The probability that agent i will be the successful contender is

$$\rho_i(x) = \rho_i(x_1, \ldots, x_n) \tag{6.4}$$

where

$$\sum_{i=1}^{n} \rho_i(x) = 1 \tag{6.5}$$

and ρ_i is nondecreasing in x_i and nonincreasing in x_j, $j \neq i$.

To evaluate the resource cost of policy contestability, we require a specification for the probability function $\rho_i(x)$. Let the political contest be perfectly discriminating in assigning the prize to the individual making the greatest outlay. If more than one contender makes the highest outlay, the prize is shared.

The model encompasses 'rent seeking' where agents contest a prespecified prize such as a quota rent, and contests for the transfer of income where the losers provide the source of the gain to the winners, as is the case with protectionist policies. In the latter case losers transfer a sum L_i to the winners as well as possibly having made outlays in unsuccessfully contesting the policy outcome.

Not all agents need be active in a contest. If agent i chooses to be inactive, in a transfer contest he nevertheless unavoidably incurs the loss L_i. Therefore this loss in his reservation payoff.

It can readily be confirmed that there exists no equilibrium in pure strategies for perfectly discriminating contests. For if agent i adopts the pure strategy of outlaying β, the probability that a rival agent j wins rises discontinuously as a function of x_j at $x_j = \beta$. Therefore there is some $\varepsilon > 0$ such that agent j will bid in the interval $[\beta - \varepsilon, \beta]$ with zero probability, for all $j \neq i$. But then agent i is better off spending $(\beta - \varepsilon)$ rather than β since his probability of winning is the same. Hence the pure strategy $x_i = \beta$ cannot be an equilibrium strategy.

A similar argument establishes that only one active agent can bid zero with positive probability. For if agent i bids zero with positive probability, any other agent increases his probability of winning discontinuously by a bid greater than zero.

Each active agent's equilibrium strategy is therefore a mixed strategy. More precisely, each active agent's spending level is a realization from a distribution with cumulative distribution function $G_i(x_i)$, where G_i is continuous over $(0, \infty)$, $G_i(0)$ is strictly positive for at most one active agent, and the minimum spending level is zero for each agent.

6.5. Contesting an income transfer

Consider now the case of a contest which involves an income transfer between two agents. If agent 1 spends x_1, his expected payoff is

$$U_1 = \left\{\begin{matrix} \text{probability} \\ \text{of winning} \end{matrix}\right\}\left\{\begin{matrix} \text{value as} \\ \text{winner} \end{matrix}\right\} - \left\{\begin{matrix} \text{probability} \\ \text{of losing} \end{matrix}\right\}\left\{\begin{matrix} \text{payment} \\ \text{as loser} \end{matrix}\right\} - x_1$$

$$= \rho_1 W_1 - (1 - \rho_1)L_1 - x_1$$

$$= -L_1 + v_1\rho_1 - x_1, \tag{6.6}$$

where

$$v_1 \equiv W_1 + L_1.$$

The amount v_i is the *gross value* to agent i of securing the policy decision in his favor relative to the option of remaining inactive.

Let agents be ranked according to their gross values, such that v_1 exceeds v_2.

Since agent 2 spends x_1 or less with probability $G_2(x_1)$, the expected payoff of agent 1 is

$$U_1(x_1) = -L_1 + G_2(x_1)v_1 - x_1. \tag{6.7}$$

Symmetrically, agent 2's expected payoff is

$$U_2(x_2) = -L_2 + G_1(x_2)v_2 - x_2. \tag{6.8}$$

Since G_1 and G_2 are continuous over $(0, \infty)$, if x^* is the maximum spending level for agent 1, agent 2 wins with probability 1 if he spends x^*. Hence agent 2 will never spend strictly more than x^*. This same argument establishes that the highest spending level of agent 2 cannot be less than that of agent 1. For if it were, agent 1 would be overspending. Since, in equilibrium, each outlay x_i must yield the same expected payoff it follows that

$$U_1(x_1) = -L_1 + G_2(x_1)v_1 - x_1 = -L_1 + v_1 - x^*, \qquad x_1 \in \text{supp}\{x\}$$

(6.9)

and

$$U_2(x_2) = -L_2 + G_1(x_2)v_2 - x_2 = -L_2 + v_2 - x^*, \qquad x_2 \in \text{supp}\{x\}.$$

(6.10)

Clearly agent 2 will never spend more than v_2. Therefore agent 1 can guarantee himself almost the entire difference $(v_1 - v_2)$ by spending a little more than v_2. If follows that agent 1 is strictly better off being active, rather than being inactive and losing L_1. Therefore, setting x_1 equal to zero in equation (6.9), we can conclude that $G_2(0)$ is strictly positive. That is, because of the threat of being completely outspent by agent 1, agent 2's strategy is to spend zero with finite probability.

At most one agent bids zero with positive probability. Therefore $G_1(0) = 0$ and, setting $x_2 = 0$ in equation (6.10), it follows that the equilibrium expected payoff of agent 2 is $-L_2$. That is, the high-valuation or strong agent pushes the low-valuation or weak agent down to the latter's reservation payoff.

Also, note that if agent 2 spends x^*, his expected payoff is $-L_2 + (v_2 - x^*)$. Therefore it must be the case that $x^* = v_2$. Solving for the equilibrium distribution functions from equations (6.9) and (6.10) reveals that with perfect discrimination and two agents whose gross valuations are v_1 and v_2 $(v_2 \leq v_1)$, the equilibrium mixed strategies are

$$G_1(x_1) = \frac{x_1}{v_2}, \qquad x_1 \in [0, v_2]$$

(6.11)

$$G_2(x_2) = \left(1 - \frac{v_2}{v_1}\right) + \frac{x_2}{v_1}, \qquad x_2 \in [0, v_2].$$

(6.12)

The expected spending levels of the two agents can then be computed to be

$$E\{x_1\} = \int_0^{v_1} x_1 \, dG_1 = \frac{1}{2} v_2 \tag{6.13}$$

$$E\{x_2\} = \int_0^{v_2} x_2 \, dG_2 = \left(\frac{v_2}{v_1}\right)\left(\frac{1}{2} v_2\right). \tag{6.14}$$

Consequently, expected total spending is

$$E\{x_1 + x_2\} = v_2\left(\frac{v_1 + v_2}{2v_1}\right). \tag{6.15}$$

For the symmetric valuation case expected outlays equal the common gross valuation v. However, under asymmetry in valuations, we observe that expected spending is lower than *either* of the gross valuations.

Now introduce a third agent with gross valuation v_3 where

$$v_3 \le v_2 \le v_1. \tag{6.16}$$

Suppose that agents 1 and 2 continue to act as in the two-agent case. Then if agent 3 spends x_3 his expected payoff is

$$U_3(x_3) = -L_3 + \mathrm{Prob}\left\{\begin{matrix} x_1 \text{ and } x_2 \\ \text{less than } x_3 \end{matrix}\right\} v_3 - x_3$$

$$= -L_3 + G_1(x_3)G_2(x_3)v_3 - x_3$$

$$= -L_3 + \frac{v_3}{v_2} x_3\left[1 - \frac{v_2}{v_1} + \frac{x_3}{v_1} - \frac{v_2}{v_3}\right]. \tag{6.17}$$

Since agent 3 will never spend more than his gross value v_3, the bracketed expression is no greater than

$$\left(1 - \frac{v_2}{v_3}\right) + \frac{(v_3 - v_2)}{v_1}.$$

Since v_3 is no greater than v_2, both expressions in parentheses are nonpositive. Thus agent 3 has no spending level that will generate a nonnegative expected payoff. His best response to the strategies of agents 1 and 2 is therefore to be inactive. Accordingly, given n agents for whom $v_1 \ge v_2 > v_3 \ge \cdots \ge v_n$, if agents 1 and 2 act as if there were no other agents, the latter have no incentive to compete.

The above is the characterization of an equilibrium of the contest. It remains to demonstrate that there is no other equilibrium; that is, that the *only* equilibrium strategy of agents 3 through n is to remain inactive. It can be shown that if, in equilibrium, there are only two active agents, it must be those two with the highest gross values. If there are $m > 2$ active agents, each must have the same gross value v and the unqiue equilibrium strategy is the symmetric equilibrium

$$G_i(x_i) = \left(\frac{x_i}{v}\right)^{\frac{1}{m-1}}. \tag{6.18}$$

It follows as a corollary that if $v_1 \geq v_2 \geq v_3 \geq \ldots v_n$ and at least one of the first two inequalities is strict, the equilibrium is unique and only agents 1 and 2 are active.

By way of contrast, with n agents who have identical gross values, there is a symmetric equilibrium with any number $m > 2$ of active agents. In particular there is an equilibrium in which only two agents are active. It is this equilibrium which the unique asymmetric equilibrium approaches as the difference in gross values declines to zero. Then, in the special case of identical valuations, the expected value of outlays mEx for any number of contenders $m \leq n$ precisely equals the common valuation v of the prize.

Asymmetric valuations therefore reduce the total value of outlays. Low valuation agents are discouraged altogether from competing against the two agents with highest valuations. The agent with the second highest valuation is also inhibited in his outlays by the knowledge that there exists an agent with a higher valuation. Agent 2 outlays zero with positive probability, but agent 1 does not win outright without a contest since agent 2 randomizes in a manner which allows for the possibility of a positive outlay. The inhibitions against lower valuation agents competing yield underdissipation with respect to v_2. However, since $v_1 = W_1 + L_1 > v_2 > W_2$, more may be spent than the value assigned to the transfer by agent 2.

Suppose that deadweight losses are the source of agents' differing valuations. Then the agent with the highest valuation incurs the lowest deadweight cost. But this agent has the greatest chance of winning. Hence the discriminating political contest biases the award of the prize to the contender incurring the least deadweight loss. Since $v_i = (W_i + L_i + D_i)$ where D_i is the deadweight cost incurred by agent i, outlays increase relative to the value of the transfer, since agents are seeking to avoid not only the payment L_i but also incurring the deadweight loss D_i.

In the special case where valuations are identical and there are no deadweight costs, it is evident that outlays necessarily exceed the value of the prize, since $mEx = v = (W + L)$ and hence $mEx > W$. The extent of overdissipation is precisely L. In the presence of a common deadweight cost D, overdissipation is $(L + D)$.

6.6. Contesting the right to a quota rent

In the case of a contest for a prespecified quota rent, $L_i = 0$. Then $v_i = W_i$, and the previous results follow for the value of the rent W_i in place of the gross valuation v_i. Only the two agents with the highest valuations W_1 and W_2 $(W_1 > W_2)$ actively compete. The reservation cost of not competing is zero. The expected utility of agent 2 who is indifferent between competing actively and remaining inactive is therefore also zero. Total spending by the two active agents is

$$E\{x_1 + x_2\} = W_2\left(\frac{W_1 + W_2}{2W_1}\right) < W_2 < W_1. \qquad (6.19)$$

The value of the political prize therefore overstates the value of outlays made, independently of which of the two agents' valuations of the prize is used.

6.7. Imperfectly discriminating contests

In an imperfectly discriminating contest, the equilibrium outcome is characterized by the designation of a probability of success for each contender, rather than actual designation of the winner. Gordon Tullock (1980) has investigated rent dissipation in such contests, which he described as "efficient rent seeking." In Tullock's contests, if individual i outlays x_i, his probability of success is $x_i^r / \sum_j x_j^r$ where the scale parameter r indicates the marginal return to lobbying outlays. All contenders have an equal valuation V of the prize, which is a predesignated rent rather than a transfer. Each individual chooses an outlay x_i to maximize expected utility given by

$$\max_{x_i \geq 0} \pi_i(x_1, \ldots, x_i, \ldots, x_n) = \frac{x_i^r}{\sum_{j=1}^n x_j^r} V - x_i. \qquad (6.20)$$

The solution in a symmetric Nash equilibrium is

$$x = r(n-1)V/n^2. \qquad (6.21)$$

From (6.21), the proportion of the rent dissipated by lobbying activity is

$$\frac{nx}{V} = \frac{r(n-1)}{n}. \qquad (6.22)$$

Overdissipation of a rent by resources expended in lobbying is inconsistent with the existence of a Nash equilibrium. The second-order condition for the problem (6.20) is

$$r \leq n/(n-2). \qquad (6.23)$$

However, choice of an outlay satisfying (6.21) and (6.23) does not ensure a global maximum. Max $\pi \geq 0$ implies $V/n - x \geq 0$, and, substituting the equilibrium value of x given by (6.21) into the latter inequality, it follows that an interior solution is a global maximum if and only if

$$r \leq n/(n-1). \qquad (6.24)$$

This implies via (6.22) that $nx \leq V$; so in a Nash equilibrium in this type of contest, contenders dissipate at most the value of the contested rent.

Tullock assumed that all contenders value the political prize equally. However, consider the consequences of asymmetric evaluation. Let individual i have a valuation v_i of the prize. To focus on the rent-seeking case considered by Tullock (as opposed to transfers), assume $L_i = 0$. Denote by $s_n(x)$ total outlays. Agent i's expected payoff from participation in a contest is

$$U_i(x) = \frac{x_i v_i}{s_n(x)} - x_i. \qquad (6.25)$$

The expected utility maximizing choice of x_i satisfies

$$\frac{\partial U_i}{\partial x_i} = \frac{(s_n - x_i)v_i}{s_n^2(x)} - 1, \qquad i = 1, \ldots, n \qquad (6.26)$$

and

$$\frac{\partial^2 U_i}{\partial x_i^2} = \frac{-2(s_n - x_i)v_i}{s_n^3(x)} < 0, \qquad i = 1, \ldots, n.$$

Therefore U_i is concave in x_i and so the first order conditions

$$\frac{\partial U_i}{\partial x_i} = \frac{(s_n - x_i)v_i}{s_n^2} - 1 = 0 \qquad i = 1, \ldots, n \qquad (6.28)$$

characterize a global interior maximum of expected utility.

Suppose that $v_1 \geq v_2 \geq v_3 \ldots \geq v_n$ and assume that all n agents actively participate in the contest. Hence $x_i > 0$, $i = 1, \ldots, n$. The harmonic mean of the n agents' valuations is

$$\bar{\bar{v}} \equiv \frac{n}{\sum_{j=1}^n \frac{1}{v_j}}. \qquad (6.29)$$

From (6.28)

$$s_n - x_i = s_n^2 \left(\frac{1}{v_i}\right). \qquad (6.30)$$

Summing over n

$$n s_n - \sum_{j=1}^n x_i = s_n^2 \left(\sum_{j=1}^n \frac{1}{v_1}\right). \qquad (6.31)$$

From the definition of s_n and $\bar{\bar{v}}$ it follows that the total value of the outlays made in the contest is

$$s_n = \left(\frac{n-1}{n}\right) \bar{\bar{v}}_n. \qquad (6.32)$$

Thus, when valuations of the political prize differ, total outlays closely approximate the harmonic mean of individuals' valuations as the number of participants increases.

Tullock investigated the symmetric case where $v_i = v$, $i = 1, \ldots, n$. In that case (6.32) reduces to

$$s_n = \left(\frac{n-1}{n}\right) v, \qquad (6.33)$$

with the common valuation v replacing the harmonic mean of valuations. A limiting complete rent-dissipation result is thus established, with respect to the common valuation v.

When evaluations differ, we cannot however presume that all agents will choose to participate actively in a contest. Consider the appearance of an $(n + 1)$th individual whose valuation of the prize is $v_{n+1} < v_n$. Suppose that the prior n individuals believe that individual $(n + 1)$ will not actively participate. The n active individuals then maintain their strategies as indicated. To establish whether this is an equilibrium given the appearance of the $(n + 1)$th individual, we need to consider the payoff to entry of the latter individual. Since $U_i(x_i)$ is concave in x_i, whether the $(n + 1)$th individual can increase his payoff by actively participating hinges on the sign of

$$\frac{\partial U_{n+1}}{\partial x_{n+1}}(x_1, \ldots, x_n, 0) = \frac{(s_{n+1} - x_{n+1})}{s_{n+1}^2} v_{n+1} - 1$$

$$= \frac{v_{n+1}}{s_n} - 1. \qquad (6.34)$$

Hence agent $(n + 1)$ will remain inactive if and only if $v_{n+1} < s_n$. Substituting from (6.32) indicates that agent $(n + 1)$ will remain inactive if and only if $v_{n+1} < (1 - 1/n)\bar{v}_n$.

As in the limiting polar case of perfect discrimination, the number of agents actively participating in Tullock's imperfectly discriminating contests will be small unless valuations are very similar. Given the small numbers of participants, rent dissipation will be substantially less than complete.

6.7. Contesting a protectionist proposal

In an imperfectly discriminating contest, consider now a protectionist proposal which yields agent 1 who is the beneficiary of protection a gain of W, which is the loss in income incurred by $(n - 1)$ agents. The gainers and losers from protection thus place asymmetric valuations on the protectionist proposal. The asymmetric valuations are $v_1 = W$ and $v_j = W/(n - 1)$, $j \geq 2$. Probabilities of winning the political contest to decide policy are

$$p_1(x) = \frac{x_1}{x_1 + y} \quad \text{where} \quad y = \sum_{j=1}^{n} x_j \qquad (6.35)$$

$$p_j(x) = \frac{y}{x_1 + y}, \quad j \geq 2. \qquad (6.36)$$

We can solve for x_1 and y by considering only agents 1 and 2 for whom

$$U_1(x_1) = \frac{Wx_1}{(x_1 + y)} - x_1 \qquad (6.37)$$

$$U_2(x_2) = \frac{W}{(n-1)} \frac{y}{(x_1 + y)} - x_2. \qquad (6.38)$$

The first order conditions are

$$\frac{Wy}{(x_1 + y)^2} = 1 = \frac{Wx_1}{(n-1)(x_1 + y)^2}. \qquad (6.39)$$

Hence the equilibrium outlays are

$$y = \frac{W}{n^2} \quad \text{and} \quad x_1 = \left(\frac{n-1}{n^2}\right)W. \qquad (6.40)$$

It follows that the probability that the protectionist proposal will succeed is $(n-1)/n$. Total outlays in this contest are $x_1 + y = W/n$. That is, total expenditures are only $1/n$th of the value of the transfer to agent 1.

It appears therefore that such protectionist proposals have a high probability of success. Every proposal for protection of a particular industry, considered individually, is of this type. The proposal is to transfer income to individuals whose incomes are tied to the (relative) output price of the industry which is the candidate for protection. The cost of protection is diffusely borne by others in the economy who individually have little incentive to allocate resources to defeat the protectionist proposal, because they bear a small part of the cost of the transfer. Notice that free-rider type disincentive problems generally associated with collective action are absent in this argument. No public-good attributes of collective action have been introduced.

6.8. Bibliographic notes

The general model of political contestability of rents and transfers set out in this section is based on Hillman and Riley (1987). The analysis of competitive rent dissipation under conditions of risk aversion is based on Hillman and Katz (1984). Long and Vousden

(1987) analyze the case where risk-averse agents compete for the share of a rent. Tullock's model (1980) of "efficient rent seeking" or imperfectly discriminating contests has been extended by a number of authors including Corcoran and Karels (1985), Higgins, Shughart and Tollison (1985) and Appelbaum and Katz (1986). The complete-dissipation character of the symmetric valuation equilibrium for perfectly discriminating contests was noted by Hirshleifer and Riley (1978) for the case of two contenders and established more generally for any number of contenders with and without fixed costs of participation by Hillman and Samet (1987). For a model of contestable rents encompassing hierarchical organization, see Hillman and Katz (1987). Some estimates of the value of the prizes associated with successful quests for protection are provided by Baldwin (1984).

7. POLITICAL CHOICE OF THE MEANS OF PROTECTION

We now move to a consideration of choice of the means of protection. Protection can take various forms. Imports can be restricted via specific and ad-valorem tariffs, import quotas, quota-tariff combinations, variable import levies, voluntary export restraints, domestic content requirement schemes, government purchasing restrictions, and various other non-tariff barriers that in subtle and not so subtle ways increase the cost of imports relative to domestically produced substitutes. Protection as a political decision encompasses choice among the various available instruments. Just as political motives can underlie the determination of levels of protection, so such motives can influence the means of protection that are chosen.

If the choice of the instrument of protection is to be of any consequence, asymmetries must be identified in the effects of different instruments. With competitive markets and no uncertainty, full equivalence prevails between the basic price and quantity means of trade intervention, tariffs and quotas, in the sense that the price, quantities consumed and domestically supplied, and the level of imports in a tariff equilibrium can be duplicated by a quota. The non-equivalence between tariffs and quotas that arise in the presence of imperfectly competitive markets and uncertainty can on the other hand influence the politically endogenous determination of choice of the means of protection. Another potential influence on instrument choice is information asymmetry. We begin with the latter commonly proposed explanation for political choice of the means of protection.

7.1. Transparency and information asymmetry

The transparency or information asymmetry argument explaining choice of the means of protection rests on the proposition that some instruments are more transparent, or more conspicuous, in their protective effects than others. In particular, if is often suggested that the protective effect of a quantitative restriction is not immediately discernable to the losers from protectionist policies, whereas a tariff provides an explicit expression of the increase in domestic price over the world price due to protection. By making the extent of the losses incurred by the losers from protection less transparent, a quantitative restriction facilitates provision of benefits to the gainers from protection in a politically less costly manner than a tariff. An example is provided by the means of restriction of U.S. auto imports. While the U.S. government imposes but a small tariff on imports of automobiles, imports of Japanese autos have been subject to quantitative restriction via voluntary export restraints. This form of trade restriction is examined in more detail in Section 8. It has been estimated that voluntary export restraints have considerably increased domestic U.S. prices of Japanese auto imports, and via substitution in domestic consumption U.S. automobile prices generally. The quantity constraint on Japanese automobile imports would appear to have resulted in quality upgrading of imports. There has also been substitution in domestic consumption towards imported pick-up trucks not subject to restraints. Consequently, the computation of the cost of the quantitative restrictions to the U.S. consumer becomes a complex econometric exercise. The statistical techniques encompass an hedonic index to correct for endogenous quality change and yield a substantially more qualified value for the cost of protection of the U.S. automobile industry via voluntary export restraints than a simple statement in a tariff schedule indicating the required payment to the Treasury for the right to purchase an imported automobile at the price offered by the foreign supplier.

A similar transparency argument is often made with respect to the choice between tariffs and tax-subsidy instruments of intervention.

The domestic effects of a tariff can be precisely duplicated by the combination of an equal percentage subsidy to domestic producers of the good protected by the tariff and tax on domestic consumption of the same good. A policy objective of influencing domestic income distribution via regulation of output prices can therefore be achieved by production subsidies which change relative prices confronting domestic producers (as do tariffs) without the consumption inefficiency incurred with a tariff. Tariffs are thus inefficient instruments for effecting income transfers when lump-sum financed production subsidies are feasible. An additional deadweight cost (the consumption cost of the tariff) is avoided by the use of production subsidies, to the advantage of both gainers and losers from a government's transfer policy. Given that re-distribution is to take place, there should presumptively be a consensus for minimizing the associated deadweight loss by using a lump-sum financed production subsidy and (abstracting from strategic use of the tariff to exploit or counter international monopoly or monopsony power) a zero tariff. However, this assumes awareness by affected individuals of the correspondence between a tariff and its tax/subsidy components.

A well-documented example of a recommendation for a tariff based on the assumption that this relationship between policy instruments is not understood is the 1929 Brigden Report on the Australian tariff. The policy objective was to encourage immigration of labor, by protecting relatively labor-intensive domestic manufacturing industry. The Brigden Report acknowledged that a production subsidy (or bounty) could encourage domestic industry to expand, thereby increasing demand for labor. However, a tariff, though more costly in efficiency terms, was proposed to achieve the objective of encouraging expansion of domestic manufacturing industry in a circuitous, less obvious manner than direct payment of subsidies. The Report concluded that therefore a tariff was politically feasible, a subsidy not.

The Brigden policy preference was strongly criticized by neo-classical economists. Jacob Viner (1929) viewed the Brigden recommendation that the tariff be maintained as

... unexpected when coming from economists who exhibit intimate acquaintance with the fundamental arguments of the free-trade economists and a sincere desire to give to these arguments all the weight to which they are entitled, who minimize the importance of the infant industry argument, who refrain in general from resorting to short-run considerations in favor of protection, and who endeavor to confine their analysis to considerations which are economic in character.

The Brigden recommendation for a tariff was based on none of the considerations raised by Viner, but on information asymmetry. Underlying such asymmetry is "rational ignorance". As previously noted (section 4.1), rational individuals may lack the incentive to become informed on issues when they can only influence outcomes by voting, since the probability of any one individual's being decisive at the polls is small. Yet in the Brigden case the "rational ignorance" argument appears inappropriate. For after all the Report was a public document. By perusal of the document, the electorate at large could learn that a more efficient means than the tariff was available for achieving the government's domestic income distribution and immigration objectives. Indeed, the longer-term outcome was "protection all-round": the domestic agricultural interests who were disadvantaged by protection secured compensation via explicit subsidies or subsidies implicit in price-support schemes.

A transparency explanation of instrument choice relies on sustained rational ignorance for the information asymmetry to persevere. Rational ignorance can be sustained by sufficiently complex administrative procedures for the provision of protection. Finger, Hall and Nelson (1982) emphasize this point with respect to the U.S. trade laws (see Section 10 for elaboration) and provide the example that dumping is defined by 300 lines of text in the antidumping act plus 1000 Federal Register lines of administrative regulations.

A formalization of the transparency explanation of instrument choice has been proposed by Steven Magee (1988). Magee suggests that instrument choice is governed by a "principle of optimal obfuscation" which leads tariffs to be chosen in preference to more efficient tax/subsidy means of intervention. Magee proposes that policymakers optimize by choosing the degree of obfuscation to trade off political costs and benefits of instrument choice. Policy obfuscation yields a political gain by making income transfers less detectable by the losers from intervention. However, there is a loss from increased obfuscation via decreased political support, since the less efficient policy instrument incurs higher deadweight costs and thereby leaves less to be distributed to the gainers from intervention. The "optimal degree of obfuscation" balances these countervailing influences.

7.2. Institutional influences

The form that protection takes is subject to the institutional arrangements which govern the conduct of a country's international trade policy. In the U.S. the national trade laws provide administrative tracks that can be taken by industries seeking protection and specify possibilities in terms of instrument choice.

Protection can also be sought by appeal to the legislative or executive branches of government. Legislative action to secure tariff or quota protection requires the fostering of protectionist sentiment sufficiently broad to win the support of majorities in both houses of Congress. In the event of a Presidential veto, the passage of the sought-after protectionist legislation requires a two-thirds congressional majority for a veto override. Substantial lobbying effort is therefore required on this track, with no assurance of ultimate success. However, unless explicitly limited in duration, protection once established via legislative action, in the U.S. or in parliamentary systems, has a permanence which can be overridden only by the introduction of new legislation to override the old.

The executive acting on its own can take action outside of the frame of reference of the national trade laws by negotiating bilateral "voluntary trade restrictions" or "orderly marketing agreements" with foreign governments representing the interests of foreign exporters. Substantial political weight appears necessary to evoke such executive intervention. Only some half dozen U.S. industries have been successful on this track—automobiles, steel, textiles and apparel, and semiconductors, and in the agriculture natural-resource based sectors, beef, sugar, and lumber.

Choice of the instrument of protection is also influenced by international institutional arrangements. The GATT exhibits a preference for tariffs over import quotas and other non-tariff barriers, on the grounds that unlike tariffs the latter instruments do not permit expansion of trade in response to increases in domestic demand. However, precisely because GATT negotiations have succeeded in securing substantial multilateral tariff reductions, non-tariff barriers have in many instances come to replace tariffs as the means of protection.

Institutional aspects of protection are considered in more detail in Section 10.

7.3. Property rights to rents and revenues

An import quota is a valuable asset. Rights of ownership can be specified and the asset can be traded.

However, while property rights are assignable to quota rents, tariff revenue is in general not assigned on an individualistic property rights basis. Rather, the revenue derived from restricting imports via a tariff becomes part of the pool of tax proceeds secured by the Treasury, and can only be contested via the political mechanism determining government budgetary allocations in general. It has been suggested that via campaign contributions and other transfers, politicians and policymakers may secure a share in the rents which they create via trade restrictions. Insofar as this is so, the political preference is for a quota rather than a tariff.

7.4. Import-equivalent tariffs and quotas

The presumption that quotas may be politically preferred to tariffs finds further support from a comparison between the profits earned by domestic firms with market power for a given quantity of competitive imports. Profits of import-competing firms are higher when imports are competitively supplied by quota holders than when the same quantity of imports is competitively supplied subject to a tariff. The tariff allows the domestic firm no domestic price discretion: the domestic price is determined exogenously by the competitive world price and the tariff. But under a quota domestic firms do exercise price discretion. Firms can therefore make profit-maximizing price and output decisions subject to competitive supply of the allowable quantity of imports. Choice of the domestic price prevailing in the tariff equilibrium is in particular an option for the firm under the established quota. The firm can therefore fare no worse under the quota than under the import-equivalent tariff, and indeed fares strictly better under the quota.

7.5. Political-support motives and the choice between tariffs and quotas

The above considerations suggest, in the absence of institutional restraints on instrument choice, a bias in favor of the use of

quantitative restrictions over tariffs: quotas are less transparent in
their protective effects, quota rents are more readily assignable to
designated beneficiaries than tariff revenues, and at the same level
of imports quotas yield higher profits to protected domestic
import-competing producers with market power.

However, to place the comparison between tariffs and quotas on
an equal footing, assume that quota rights are competitively
auctioned and that the proceeds, as with tariff revenue, accrue to
the Treasury. Then there is no political gain from assigning quota
rights. Let the objective of the policymaker be the maximization of
political support, as expressed in terms of the political-support
function of Section 2. Policymakers are therefore assumed to
behave in a manner which trades off political support from gainers
from protection against the loss of support from those harmed by
protection. Let the gainers from protection be the residual claimants to the profits of a firm which in the absence of competitive
imports has monopoly power in the domestic market.

The political-support function which the policymaker seeks to
maximize via choice of trade policy is

$$M = M[\pi - \pi^*, P - P^*] \qquad (7.1)$$

where P^* is the free-trade competitive world price and π^* denotes
free-trade profits of the domestic firm; and π and P are respectively,
profits and domestic price subsequent to protection. Equation (7.1)
is maximized subject to the concave domestic profit function indicating the increase in profits over the free-trade level as protection
increases the domestic price above the world price:

$$\pi - \pi^* = h(P - P^*). \qquad (7.2)$$

Choice of the political-support maximizing level of protection
proceeds in the manner outlined in Section 2.

However, let the policymaker be given the further discretion of
choice between a tariff and a quota as the means of sustaining the
domestic price P above the free-trade price P^*.

Profits earned by the firm depend upon whether the policymaker
chooses a tariff or a quota. As depicted in Figure 7.1, profits are
greater under a tariff than under a quota.

This is consistent with the result which obtains for equivalent
imports, that profits are greater under a quota than under an

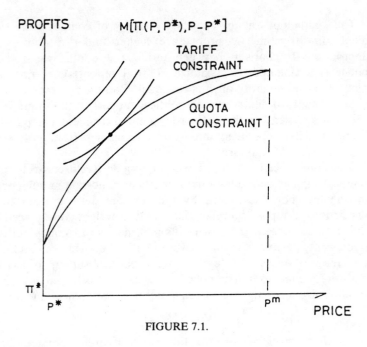

FIGURE 7.1.

import-equivalent tariff. The comparison in Figure 7.1 is not at a common quantity of imports, but at a common domestic price.

The comparative outcome portrayed in Figure 7.1, that at a domestic price between the free-trade price P^* and the domestic profit-maximizing price P^m profits are greater under the tariff, can be confirmed with reference to Figure 7.2. The price P can be sustained either via a tariff of height $(P - P^*)$ or via a quota of QT. Imports under the tariff are $FT < QT$. The quota equilibrium is established by seeking that quantity of competitively supplied imports which, when subtracted from domestic demand, yields a residual demand function subject to which the price P maximizes domestic profits. At this common domestic price, profits under the tariff exceed profits under the quota by the amount given by QFZ.

Political support is therefore maximized by the policymaker's choosing a tariff as the means of protection. The political-support equilibrium is depicted in Figure 7.1 where a contour of the political-support function $M(\cdot)$ is tangent to the tariff constraint.

Thus, although for any specified quantity of competitively supplied imports domestic profits are higher under a quota, the appropriate comparison between tariffs and quotas when trade policy is formulated to maximize political support does not take place with the quantity of imports equal. Rather, domestic price is held constant, to neutralize the political support of the losers from protection. Then, in the price-equivalent instrument comparison, profits, and hence political support from the gainers from protection, are greater under the tariff.

This dominance of the tariff over a quota derives exclusively from political-support considerations. In particular, no role in influencing instrument choice is played by the revenue derived from trade restrictions. Suppose however that political weight were placed on the revenue consequences of tariffs and quotas (assuming still that quota-rents accrue to the government). Political valuation of revenue introduces a trade-off between political-support objectives and revenue received. The policymaker can be portrayed as seeking to maximize a strictly quasiconcave political-preference function

$$V = V[M, R] \qquad (43)$$

where R is tariff revenue or the value of quota premia. Since

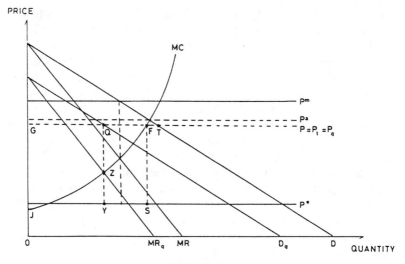

FIGURE 7.2.

political support and revenue are positively valued by the policy-maker, V_M, $V_R > 0$.

Figure 7.3 depicts the instrument-contingent constraints. From a political-support vantage the tariff is dominant, and hence maximal political-support M_t under the tariff exceeds that M_q attainable under a quota. However, the maximum revenue R_q attainable under a quota exceeds the maximum revenue R_t that can be secured via a tariff; since it can be confirmed with reference to Figure 7.2 that at any given domestic price imports are greater under the quota.

There is now no unequivocal political preference for either instrument. If sufficient weight is placed by the policymaker on the revenue derived from trade restrictions, (7.3) may (but need not) be maximized by choice of a quota as in the example depicted in Figure 7.3.

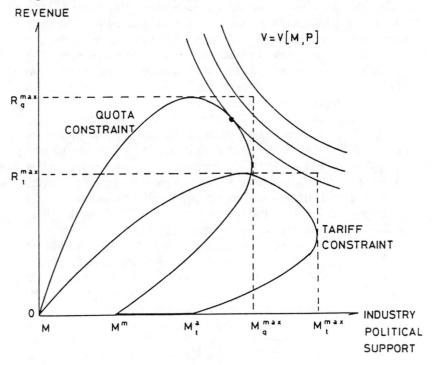

FIGURE 7.3.

7.6. Terms of trade uncertainty and the choice between tariffs and quotas

The above comparison has been based on the asymmetry between tariffs and quotas when domestic markets are not competitive. Tariffs and quotas also differ in their effects in the presence of uncertainty. To allow a focus on the implications of uncertainty, let us eliminate the source of tariff/quota asymmetry due to imperfectly competitive markets. Let uncertainty derive from randomness in an industry's exogenous world price of output P^*, and let P^* have a known distribution $h(P^*)$. A protectionist policy specified ex-ante (before the realization of P^*) transforms the distribution $h(P^*)$ into a distribution $g(P)$ where P is the protection-inclusive domestic price. The nature of the transformation from $h(P^*)$ to $g(P)$ depends upon whether the means of protection is a tariff or a quota.

Consider an ad-valorem tariff t such that $P^*(1 + t) = P$. The ad-valorem tariff results in a distribution of domestic prices $g(P)$ which provides a state-invariant rate of protection: whatever the realization P^*, the domestic price is a given percentage increase at the rate t. Thus an ad-valorem tariff transforms the distribution $h(P^*)$ to yield proportionally higher realized domestic prices in response to higher realized world prices.

A specific tariff has a different effect. The lower the realized world price, the greater the state-dependent rate of protection provided. Given a specific tariff T such that $(P^* + T) = P$, the rate of protection is $t = T/P^*$. The implicit tariff rate t thus varies inversely with the world price P^*. A specific tariff therefore effects an asymmetric transformation on $h(P^*)$ by providing greater protection, the more unfavorable is the realized world price confronting the domestic import-competing industry.

Import quotas however provide the most effective means of protection against adverse realizations of world prices. In Figure 7.4 $\bar{P}$ is the domestic market-clearing price when domestic excess demand is equal to the imports allowable under a quota GH. Should the realized world price P^* exceed $\bar{P}$, the quota is not binding and the domestic price equals the world price. On the other hand, for any realized world price below $\bar{P}$, the binding quota continues to enforce $\bar{P}$ as the domestic price: thus for example at the realized world price P_1^* excess domestic demand remains

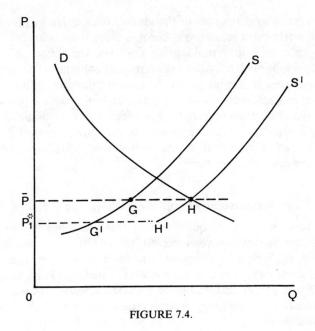

FIGURE 7.4.

$GH(=G'H')$. The quota-inclusive domestic supply function given P_1^* is S'. $\bar{P}$ remains the equilibrium domestic price. The import quota therefore truncates the distribution $h(P^*)$ at $\bar{P}$, eliminating domestic prices below $\bar{P}$ as possible outcomes.

The identical truncating effect is achieved by a system of variable import levies such as are used for protectionist purposes by the E.E.C. Under variable import levies, the domestic price of output is preset and the import duty varies with realizations of the world price to maintain the predetermined domestic price. Randomness in the world price therefore does not affect domestic prices, hence stabilizing those domestic incomes which are tied to the output prices.

Sufficient risk aversion can give rise to utility functions that are strictly concave in (relative) output prices (see Section 9). Domestic producers who are sufficiently risk-averse can thus exhibit a preference for the quota or a variable import levy over a tariff because of the elimination of downside risk of income loss by the former instruments. Similarly, a specific tariff may be preferred to an ad-valorem tariff because of the greater compensatory protective effect as world price realizations become more unfavorable.

The preferred policy ranking for domestic consumers might be quite the opposite. Under not very stringent conditions, consumers' utility is convex in output prices. Increased price variability is then beneficial to consumers. However, sufficiently risk-averse producers prefer reduced price variability. Hence, what at issue is not whether protection is to be provided but how, consumers may prefer an ad-valorem tariff, the instrument least preferred by risk-averse domestic producers.

7.7. Tariffs as the outcome of multidimensional social choice

Let us now return to the question why trade instruments are at all used to seek domestic income-redistribution objectives. An answer proposed in Section 7.1 rested on information asymmetry and rational ignorance. Another explanation, which has been proposed by Wolfgang Mayer and Raymond Riezman (1987), is based on the characteristics of majority voting equilibria when choices are multidimensional.

Consider an economy with a population differentiated by three characterstics: (i) different factor ownership, (ii) different consumption preferences, and (iii) different income tax liabilities because of different incomes. Were individuals to differ only in factor ownership, they would disagree only with regard to the value of the production tax/subsidy component of the tariff; for only this component of the tariff affects factor incomes. Majority voting could then establish an equilibrium production tax/subsidy policy which reflects the preferred policy of the median voter, in the manner described in Section 3 for determination of a tariff. However, when the additional sources of difference (ii) and (iii) among individuals are introduced, policy disagreement can range over values for both the production and the consumption tax/subsidy components of the tariff. In such a multidimensional choice space, there is in general no unique equilibrium associated with the median-voter rule. Control of the agenda determines the equilibrium policy outcome. Indeed, in principle, voting procedures can be designed that make any feasible outcome an equilibrium social choice.

Tariffs could be in the Pareto-efficient set of choices, if that set happened to include equiproportional production subsidies and consumption taxes. If a tariff were chosen, there need not exist any individual voter for whom the policy combination of production subsidy and consumption tax implicit in the tariff is individually optimal. In contrast, when disagreement is unidimensional, the collectively chosen equilibrium outcome is individually optimal for the median voter.

Multidimensionality in choice arises because of four possibly conflicting effects of tax/subsidy instruments on individual welfare. Let revenue from taxes be distributed in an unbiased manner. That is, the income distribution is unchanged by tax-revenue distribution. Then an individual gains from a consumption tax on good i if (1) his marginal propensity to consume that good is less than average. Individuals' incomes are also subject to (2) a factor income effect, as changes in relative domestic supply prices change factor incomes. With the government budget balanced, (3) a change in indirect taxation affects direct tax liabilities. In particular, if direct taxation is progressive, the relatively well-off favor indirect taxes. Individual welfare is also affected by (4) deadweight losses associated with the production and consumption tax/subsidy components of the tariff, with the burden of such deadweight losses distributed according to individuals' expenditure shares.

Every voter has individual utility-maximizing values for the production and consumption tax/subsidy components of a tariff, as determined by the individual's particular factor ownership, consumption preferences, and tax liabilities. An individual's optimal consumption tax is positive if his marginal propensity to consume the taxed good is less than average and if the decrease in direct tax liability via the substitution of the indirect tax for direct taxation is more pronounced than average. The individually optimal production tax is positive, insofar as the tax changes domestic relative prices so as to increase the individual's real factor income, the individual's tax liability declines via the indirect/direct tax substitution, and the production tax redistributes income so as to change the marginal propensity to consume of the taxed good in a manner which increases tax revenue, thereby lowering the individual's direct tax liability.

For any given values of the production and consumption

tax/subsidy instruments, it is evident that an individual may wish to vote for an increase in the production tax but reduction in the consumption tax, or vice-versa. A proposal to change a tariff would then give rise to a conflict with respect to the direction of change sought by an individual for one of the tax/subsidy components of the tariff. Only by coincidence could an equiproportional production/consumption tax/subsidy outcome implicit in a tariff be utility-maximizing for a particular voter; although in principle equiproportional production subsidies and consumption taxes and hence tariffs could be in the Pareto-efficient set of policy choices.

Tariffs emerge as the possible chosen instrument of policy under the following assumptions: suppose that because of organization costs political coalitions do not form on the basis of consumption preferences, and suppose that because of high fixed costs each individual or group confines political activity to influencing the value of but a single instrument of policy. Under these conditions, tariffs will be sought by two categories of individuals, those who experience a net gain via the production-subsidy effect on factor incomes, and those who experience a net gain because of a reduced tax burden as the consequence of the shift from direct to indirect taxation.

Of course, the relatively well-off individuals who gain from the indirect/direct tax substitution would prefer to have only the consumption tax component of the tariff implemented, since thereby more revenue would be raised from indirect taxation and the production deadweight loss of the tariff could be avoided. But coalitions based on consumption preferences are ruled out by assumption. Hence the relatively well off support the tariff.

7.8. The public-good nature of tariffs and quotas

Domestic import-competing interests are in principle indifferent between an explicit production subsidy and the subsidy implicit in a protective tariff or quota. However, tariffs and quotas provide benefits to industry interests that are in the nature of a public good. All owners of industry-specific factors benefit from protection secured via these instruments independently of the identity of the agents whose political activities underlie the protectionist response. A subsidy could on the other hand be firm-specific and thereby yield private benefits. Rodrik (1986) has compared lobbying for a tariff with public-good benefits to lobbying for a firm-specific private-benefit subsidy. Assuming that agents act independently, and all other things equal, the incentive to lobby is greater with a subsidy, for all gains from influence over policy are internalized by the beneficiaries of the lobbying activity. Since the benefits of lobbying are not entirely internalized by the beneficiaries of tariffs and quotas, fewer resources are allocated to lobbying activity when tariffs or quotas are sought, than when the source of gain to firms is a firm-specific subsidy.

7.9. Bibliographic notes

For elaboration on transparency and rational ignorance with particular reference to the Brigden position on instrument choice, see Hillman (1977). Feenstra (1984) estimates the costs to U.S. consumers of voluntary export restraints on U.S. automobiles and demonstrates now VERs obscure the cost of protection. The model of political-support maximizing choice between tariffs and quotas is based on Cassing and Hillman (1985). The analysis of the choice between tariffs and quotas under uncertainty is based on Falvey and Lloyd (1986). See Gary Becker (1983, 1985) for an argument that the observed use of an instrument is presumptively efficient, because of the interest of both gainers and losers from income redistribution in minimizing deadweight losses.

8. FOREIGN INTERESTS: THE ROLE FOR VOLUNTARY EXPORT RESTRAINTS

8.1. The foreign interest in the means of protection

This section considers voluntary export restraints (VERs) as instruments of trade policy. VERs are quantitative restrictions on international trade. However, when a VER is used as a protective device, the rents from the restriction of international trade accrue to the foreign suppliers of the restricted imports. Thus, in comparison with domestically assigned import quotas, foreigners gain from VERs. Foreigners also have reason to prefer VERs to tariffs, since the revenue from restriction of trade via a tariff accrues to the home government. The use of VERs in place of the more traditional tariff and quota instruments of trade restriction accordingly suggests a political response favoring foreign interests. Since foreigners benefit from VERs relative to other instruments, an explanation for the use of VERs suggestively encompasses the role that foreign interests might play in influencing the domestic determination of international trade policy.

8.2. Preemption

One view of VERs is that such trade restrictions are voluntarily agreed to by foreigners in order to preempt the unilateral imposition of protectionist policies by governments in export markets. Viewed as such, VERs are indeed voluntary, relative to the alternative threatened trade restriction. However, VERs are also on this view involuntary, in that in the absence of protectionist pressures in foreign markets the government in the exporting country would not constrain the foreign sales of its domestic firms.

A role for intervention by the government in the exporting country encompasses here regulation to address a free-rider problem. The likelihood that trade restrictions will be unilaterally imposed in the export market may increase with aggregate industry exports. An individual firm will not internalize the effect of a marginal increase in its exports on the expected loss incurred by other firms if unilateral trade restrictions are imposed in export markets.

The preemption argument has also been made in terms of cultural characteristics. VERs prominently involve Japanese exports. It has been suggested that VERs may reflect a preference for undertaking unpleasant unavoidable acts oneself rather than leave the execution to others.

8.3. Compensation

VERs have also been viewed as reflecting compensation to foreigners for denial of domestic market access. The compensation takes the form of the transfer of the rents due to the trade restriction.

There are two, albeit related, reasons for the compensatory transfer. The government that has imposed the trade restriction may wish to forestall retaliation by foreign governments. The compensatory transfer may achieve this by ameliorating the foreign losses due to restricted access to the domestic market. Relatedly, the government imposing the trade restriction may feel obliged to provide foreigners with compensation because the restriction of trade is in conflict with prior negotiated commitments. The process of trade liberalization in general entails the exchange of concessions whereby governments agree to allow each others' producers access (under specified conditions) to each others' markets (see Section 10). In imposing trade restrictions, governments may be violating their sides of such market-access agreements. The rent transfer via the VER provides compensation for violation of the contractual trade-liberalization agreement.

A formalization of the compensation aspect of VERs views such trade restrictions as components of incentive-compatible trade policies which provide the restriction-imposing government with no incentive to overstate the domestic political pressure for protection. The envisioned scenario is that in order to achieve political gain by increase in political support, domestic policymakers will wish to respond favorably to domestic protectionist pleas, in violation of contractual trade-liberalization agreements. There is asymmetric information, in that foreigners can only perceive imperfectly the political pressure to which domestic policymakers find themselves subjected in making trade policy decisions. Hence, political-support maximizing policymakers can, and have an incentive to, overstate the political pressure to which they are subject, if foreigners accept the plea of force majeure in the determination of domestic trade policy. VERs constitute in this setting side payments to foreigners which inhibit the overstatement of domestic protectionist pressures and allow the formulation of incentive-compatible trade restrictions.

8.4. Mutual gain

Both the preemption and compensation perspectives on VERs suppose that export restraints are involuntary, in that foreign exporters would prefer continued free trade to a restriction in any form on their export sales. It has however been observed that foreigners may gain from an enforced restriction of export sales. The restriction may facilitate a profit-maximizing equilibrium for foreign exporters that more closely approximates the collusive joint-profit maximizing equilibrium than free trade. Since domestic import-competing interests gain from a reduction in competitive imports, a VER can accordingly be a source of mutual gain for domestic and foreign interests. In that case, a VER is indeed voluntary. The home government, in conjunction with the foreign government, imposes a regulatory equilibrium which advantages producers at home and abroad.

If a VER increases the joint profits of foreign exporters, then presumptively the foreign exporters could themselves have restrained their exports to increase profits. However, such collusion by firms in the foreign export industry would be in violation of trade laws. A restriction of exports at the initiative of the home government in the consuming economy does not confront this problem. The regulatory equilibrium is moreover enforced by the exporting country's government, which monitors adherence to the restrictive trade agreement to assure that no exporting firm exceeds its quota of sales in the importing economy.

8.5. Foreign interests and domestic politics

The incentive of foreign interests to influence the conduct of domestic trade policy can be portrayed in a model of political competition between candidates for elective office who formulate trade policies to maximize their probabilities of election, and whose policy positions are influenced by political support from domestic and foreign producer interests. Let foreign interests be portrayed as the residual claimants to profits in the foreign export industry, which is composed of m identical Cournot firms. The foreign firms thus choose domestic sales noncooperatively, unless directed otherwise by the terms of a VER agreement. Domestic interests are portrayed by n domestic firms which abide by domestic antitrust laws and refrain from collusive activities.

Foreigners cannot directly influence trade policy by voting in domestic political contests. Under representative democracy, however, campaign contributions can be provided to a favored candidate, or other transfers can be made directed at influencing the trade policy position taken by a political candidate.

Assume that campaign contributions to a favored candidate are chosen by firms to maximize expected profits, which depend upon the rival candidates' prospects for election and upon the trade policy to which a candidate commits himself if elected. The campaign contributions made by firms have a public-good character. Any one firm's outlays benefit via political support other firms in the industry.

The domestic import-competing industry produces a homogenous good which is however imperfectly substitutable in domestic consumption for imports provided by foreign firms. Domestic demand functions for the domestic good and imports are respectively

$$P = a - bx + \gamma P^* \tag{8.1}$$

$$P^* = a - bx^* + \gamma P \tag{8.2}$$

where x and x^* denote quantities of domestically produced and foreign goods, and P and P^* are the respective domestic prices of the two goods; γ, which is a constant with values $0 \le \gamma < 1$, measures substitutability in consumption between domestic and foreign goods. If $\gamma = 0$, demand for each good depends only upon its own price, reflecting zero substitutability.

Each of the n domestic firms makes a campaign contribution L_i to influence the outcome of an electoral contest between two candidates, one of whom is predisposed to a protectionist and the other to a liberal trade policy. Firms' per unit production costs are a constant c. A domestic firm chooses output and a campaign contribution to the protectionist candidate to maximize profits given by

$$\max_{x_i, L_i} \pi_i = (P - c)x_i - L_i, \qquad i = 1, \ldots, n. \tag{8.3}$$

The foreign industry likewise seeks to influence domestic trade policy. Foreign firms have the same per unit cost of production as domestic firms. If a tariff t is the means of trade intervention, the profit-maximization problem confronting a foreign firm is

$$\max_{x_i^*, L_i^*} \pi_i^* = (P^* - c - t)x_i^* - L_i^*, \qquad i = 1, \ldots, m. \tag{8.4}$$

Alternatively, with an export restraint, foreign firms maximize profits subject to

$$x_i^* \le V/m \tag{8.5}$$

where V is the maximal permissible quantity of exports.

Each candidate seeks to maximize his probability of election, which is determined by campaign contributions received relative to total contributions. The protectionist candidate, who is the beneficiary of domestic firms' contributions, thus seeks to maximize

$$W = \frac{L}{L + L^*} \qquad (8.6)$$

where $L = \sum_{i=1}^{n} L_i$ and $L^* = \sum_{i=1}^{m} L_i^*$. The candidate predisposed to a liberal trade policy conversely seeks to minimize W.

8.6. A reference case: political competition with a tariff

For comparison with a VER, let candidates' policy pronouncements first be made in terms of a tariff. Firms choose domestic sales as symmetric Nash equilibria ex-post, after the determination of the successful candidate and the implementation of that candidate's announced tariff policy. The Nash-equilibrium outputs imply the respective profit functions for domestic and foreign firms,

$$\pi_i(t) = \frac{1}{\beta(1 - \gamma^2)A^2} \{[m(1 - \gamma) + 1]B + (1 - \gamma^2)\gamma mt\}^2 \qquad (8.7)$$

$$\pi_i^*(t) = \frac{1}{\beta(1 - \gamma^2)A^2} \{[n(1 - \gamma) + 1]B - (n + 1)(1 - \gamma^2)t\}^2 \qquad (8.8)$$

where $A \equiv (m + 1)(n + 1) - mn\gamma^2 > 0$ and $B \equiv (1 + \gamma)(a - c(1 - \gamma)) > 0$. For non-prohibitive tariffs, (8.7) and (8.8) indicate that profits of domestic and foreign firms are respectively strictly increasing and decreasing convex functions of the tariff.

Domestic and foreign interests perceive the dependence via (8.7) and (8.8) of profits on the tariff and make campaign contributions to influence the political candidates' tariff pronouncements. Firms choose their contributions as Nash equilibria. The outlays made reflect the public-good nature of campaign contributions and are a deduction from ex-post profits given by (8.7) and (8.8).

When deciding on campaign contributions, firms confront the uncertainty of not knowing which candidate will be elected. Firms are risk-neutral and choose campaign contributions to maximize expected profits. For a domestic firm, expected profits are

$$E\pi_i = \Pr\{0\}[\pi_i(t_0) - L_i] + \Pr(1)[\pi_i(t_1) - L_i]$$
$$= \Pr\{0\}\pi_i(t_0) + \Pr\{1\}\pi_i(t_1) - L_i \qquad (8.9)$$

where $\Pr\{0\}$ and $\Pr\{1\}$ are the respective probabilities of election of the liberal trade policy and protectionist candidates, and t_0 and t_1 ($t_0 \le t_1$) are the candidates' respective tariff pronouncements. The expected profits of a foreign firm, $E\pi_i^*$, likewise encompass the two states of the world described by the policy pronouncements of the rival candidates, and take the same form as (8.9).

Campaign contributions determine the candidates' probabilities of electoral success, via

$$\Pr(0) = L^*/(L + L^*) \equiv W(L, L^*)$$
$$\Pr(1) = L/(L + L^*) \equiv 1 - W(L, L^*) \qquad (8.10)$$

where L and L^* are as defined in (8.6) total contributions by domestic and foreign firms.

Substituting (8.10) into (8.9) establishes that the expected-profit maximizing campaign contribution of a domestic firm satisfies

$$\frac{\partial E\pi_i}{\partial L_i} = \frac{L^*}{(L + L^*)^2}[\pi_i(t_1) - \pi_i(t_0)] - 1 = 0, \qquad i = 1, \ldots, n, \quad (8.11)$$

Hence,

$$\frac{L^*}{(L + L^*)^2}\Delta\pi_i = 1, \qquad i = 1, \ldots, n \qquad (8.11')$$

where $\Delta\pi_i \equiv [\pi_i(t_1) - \pi_i(t_0)]$ is the difference in domestic firms' profits for the states associated with the rival candidates' tariff pronouncements.

For foreign firms, the expected-profit maximizing choice of campaign contributions satisfies a similar condition

$$\frac{L}{(L + L^*)^2}\Delta\pi_i^* = 1, \qquad i = 1, \ldots, m. \qquad (8.12)$$

Combining (8.11') and (8.12) yields the relationship between equilibrium campaign contributions

$$\frac{L}{L^*} = \frac{\Delta\pi_i}{\Delta\pi_i^*} = \frac{\pi_i(t_1) - \pi_i(t_0)}{\pi_i^*(t_0) - \pi_i^*(t_1)} \equiv R(t_0, t_1). \qquad (8.13)$$

Candidates choose the tariff pronouncements t_0 and t_1 to maximize their respective probabilities of electoral success. The protectionist candidate seeks to maximize $\Pr(1) = L/(L + L^*)$, which entails maximizing $R(t_0, t_1)$ as defined in (8.13). Hence, maximization of the protectionist candidate's probability of electoral success implies choice of a tariff which maximizes $\Delta\pi_i/\Delta\pi_i^*$, the state-contingent difference in profits of domestic firms relative to foreign firms.

The relationship (8.13) therefore ties together candidates' political motives and firms' profit-maximizing market objectives. Each candidate has a political interest in maximizing the gains which his constituency secures from his announced policy relative to the gains which his opponent's constituency secures from the opponent's policy.

Since a candidate's choice of tariff pronouncement influences the profits that both domestic and foreign firms would earn on his election, an increase in the tariff proposed by the protectionist candidate may increase $\Delta\pi_i$, but at the same time many also increase $\Delta\pi_i^*$. It cannot therefore be presupposed that the protectionist candidate will announce a prohibitive tariff or that his rival will announce a policy of free trade. It can, however, be demonstrated that such is the outcome of political competition with a tariff. Each candidate announces that policy which maximizes the profits of his constituency and minimizes the profits of his rivals' constituency. A tariff equilibrium is thus politically and economically divisive.

To confirm that this is the nature of a tariff equilibrium, assume that $t_0 < t_1$ and evaluate $\Delta\pi_i$ and $\Delta\pi_i^*$. Substitution into (8.13) yields an expression for $R(t_0, t_1)$ which is strictly increasing in t_0 and t_1. Hence the protectionist candidate can increase his probability of election by announcing increasingly greater tariffs, up to the autarkic (Nash) tariff, while the liberal trade-policy candidate has the converse incentive to announce increasingly smaller tariffs, up to free trade. If the candidates announce the same tariff, probabilities of election are equal, since nothing distinguishes the candidates. Then in (8.13) $W = R/(1 + R) = 1/2$. An equilibrium with common tariff pronouncements is however unstable. At least one candidate can improve his election prospects by deviating from the common pronouncement. A common interior Hotelling-type platform is thus not a stable equilibrium. The equilibrium policy platform is that where each candidate takes the extreme position, autarky or free trade, associated with the interests of his constituency.

Market structure in the domestic import-competing and foreign export industries, as characterized by the respective values of n and m, and substitutability as measured by γ between imports and domestic goods, together determine the candidates' probabilities of election. Denote by $\bar{t}$ the prohibitive tariff. Figure 8.1 depicts three contours (which are necessarily increasing and non-interesecting) along which $R(0, \bar{t}) = 1$ and hence along which free trade and protectionist outcomes are equally likely. As the substitution parameter γ increases, the protectionist candidate's probability of election increases for given market-structure characteristics. The more substitutable are domestically produced goods for imports, the greater the gain to domestic firms from protection relative to free trade, and hence the greater the incentive to make campaign

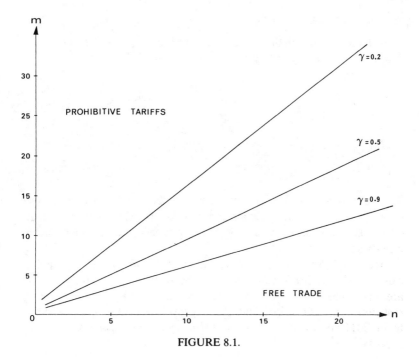

FIGURE 8.1.

contributions to the protectionist candidate. At the same time, foreign firms have less to lose from a denial of access to the domestic market as γ increases, and make smaller campaign contributions to their candidate.

Increased competition, whether in terms of more competitors in a firm's own industry or abroad, decreases firms' profits, but *ceteris paribus* profits are decreased more by increased competitiveness in a firm's own industry, since domestic goods and imports are imperfectly substitutable. As competition increases, profits fall, and the voluntary public-good outlays on campaign contributions fall. An increase in the number of domestic firms therefore reduces the benefits to domestic firms from a protectionist outcome by more than the reduction in benefit to foreign firms from a free-trade outcome. Hence, in Figure 8.1, for given γ, an increase in n holding m constant increases the probability of election of the free-trade candidate.

8.7. Voluntariness of VERs

Now let trade restrictions take the form of VERs. Foreign firms' profits subject to a binding export constraint

$$x_i^* = V/m \tag{8.19}$$

are

$$\pi_i^*(V) = \frac{V}{m(n+1)(1-\gamma^2)}[(n(1-\gamma)+1)B - b(n(1-\gamma^2)+1)V]. \tag{8.20}$$

Since $\partial \pi_i^*/\partial V \gtreqless 0$, foreign profits may either increase or decrease as an export restraint is marginally relaxed. We may regard an export restraint as voluntary if profits increase, and as involuntary otherwise.

Figure 8.2 depicts the two forms that the foreign profit function can take. If the profit function is of the form OHG, foreign profits are maximized when exports are unconstrained, and any export restraint is therefore involuntary. However, a profit function of the form OJH allows foreign profits to be increased by a restriction of exports.

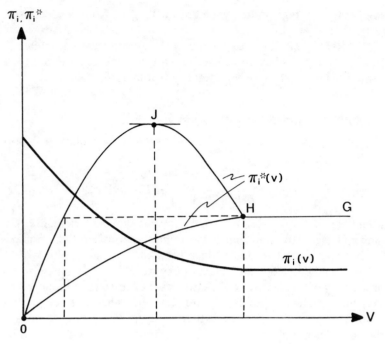

FIGURE 8.2.

From (8.20) an export restraint can be voluntary only if

$$m > \frac{n+1}{n(1-\gamma^2)+1}. \tag{8.21}$$

Should this condition hold, foreign and domestic firms have a common interest in supporting a policy of some restriction of trade via a VER.

The RHS of (8.21) exceeds unity as long as there is some substitutability in domestic consumption between domestic and foreign goods ($\gamma > 0$). (8.21) therefore confirms that if the foreign industry were to consist of a single firm or were collusively organized as a joint profit-maximizing cartel ($m = 1$), an export restraint could only be involuntary. Given n and γ, increases in m and consequently more competitive foreign industry structures can make an initially involuntary export restraint voluntary. The more competitive foreign industry has more to gain from the collusive restriction of exports.

The RHS of (8.21) is increasing in the substitution parameter γ. Hence, as imports become closer substitutes for domestic output, a restraint can switch from voluntary to involuntary.

8.8. Political competition with export restraints

The profit function of domestic firms subject to a binding export restraint is

$$\pi_i(V) = \frac{1}{b(n+1)^2(1-\gamma^2)} [B - b\gamma V]^2, \qquad (8.22)$$

where $\partial \pi_i / \partial V < 0$, $\partial^2 \pi_i / V^2 > 0$. Hence, as depicted in Figure 8.2, max $\pi_i(V) = \pi_i(0)$, confirming that domestic firms' profits are maximized by an export restraint which prohibits competitive imports.

Each candidate chooses a level of export restraint to maximize his probability of election. Let V_1 be the level of restraint announced by the protectionist candidate, and let the liberal trade policy candidate announce V_0, where then $V_0 \geq V_1$. The relation between the candidates' political objectives and firms' profits is described by

$$\frac{L}{L^*} = \frac{\Delta \pi_i}{\Delta \pi_i^*} \equiv R(V_0, V_1) \qquad (8.23)$$

where $\Delta \pi_i$ and $\Delta \pi_i^*$ are derived from the profit functions (8.20) and (8.22).

The protectionist candidate chooses V_1 to maximize $R(V_0, V_1)$ and the liberal trade-policy candidate chooses V_0 to minimize $R(V_0, V_1)$. The outcome of such political competition is the announcement of a common policy. That is, in contrast with the tariff, policy pronouncements converge. In particular, the convergence can result in an interior equilibrium for V that increases the profits of both foreign and domestic producers.

The proof of convergence in the case of VERs is similar to that of divergence in the case of a tariff. In (8.23), suppose that $V_0 > V_1$. $R(V_0, V_1)$ is increasing in both V_0 and V_1. The liberal trade-policy candidate thus improves his election prospects by decreasing V_0 while the protectionist candidate has the converse incentive to increase V_1. Hence, when policy pronouncements differ, the candidates converge in their policies. The common policy towards which candidates' pronouncements converge is a unique stable equilibrium.

Whether the unique equilibrium yields an export restraint that can be mutually beneficial to producer interests is determined by whether in an interior equilibrium the condition (8.21) holds. However, even if (8.21) is not satisfied so that foreign producers lose from the restriction of trade, an interior VER equilibrium is conciliatory, in that the level of export restraint is less than that sought by domestic producer interests. Foreign producers fare better than they would have done, had trade policy exclusively accommodated the interests of domestic producers.

Comparative statistics properties of export-restraint equilibria are described in Figure 8.3. In region 1 the equilibrium export restraint is prohibitive, whereas in regions 2 and 3 the equilbrium policy allows exports. Given n, the outcome is free trade (region 3) if m is

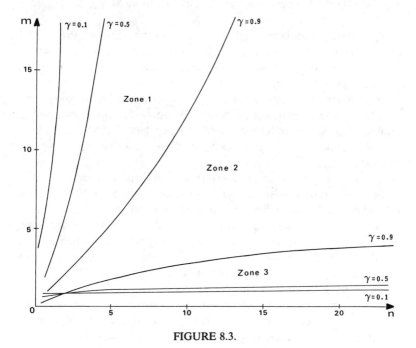

FIGURE 8.3.

sufficiently small. In region 2 of interior equilibria, $\partial V/\partial m < 0$, and hence the equilibrium export restraint becomes more stringent the more competitive is the foreign export industry. Also, since $\partial V/\partial n > 0$, the equilibrium level of export restraint is conversely less stringent, the more competitive is the domestic import-competing industry.

The boundaries in Figure 8.3 are determined by substitutability between domestic goods and imports. As γ decreases, regions 1 and 3 diminish and region 2 which is consistent with the interior solutions correspondingly expands. Region 1 diminishes because with decreased substitutability between imports and foreign goods a restriction on imports has less value for domestic firms. In the limit as $\gamma \to 0$, domestic firms have no interest in making outlays to inhibit imports, and hence region 1 disappears. Foreign firms continue to have an incentive to influence trade policy. Indeed, as γ falls, the gain to foreign firms from domestic market access increases. Foreign firms lobby for the collusive foreign-profit maximizing export restraint. Hence in the limit as $\gamma \to 0$, region 3 also disappears.

Now allow candidates discretion in choosing between tariffs and export restraints. When the choice is available of making policy pronouncements in terms of either instrument, both candidates choose export restraints.

The export restraint is the equilibrium instrument of policy without regard for market structure in the domestic import-competing and foreign export industries, and independently of the degree of substitutability in domestic consumption between imports and domestic goods.

It is to be expected that in a political equilibrium export restraints rather than tariffs arise as the instruments adopted by the rival candidates' to make policy pronouncements. Rival candidates place no value on revenue that might derive from a tariff, since such revenue accrues to the general fund of government receipts to which the candidates have no claim. However, while the candidates have no means of appropriating or benefitting from the revenue from a tariff that they might propose, there is a prospective benefit from the rents transferred to firms by export restraints. The latter rents, whether secured by foreign or domestic firms, can be transformed via the political process (if only partially) into campaign contributions, thereby affecting the candidates' ultimate concern, their probabilities of attaining political office.

In the above consideration of political candidates' choices between tariffs and quantitative restrictions, export restraints have been compared with tariffs to the exclusion of auctioned import quotas. Unlike the rents due to VER's but like tariff revenue, the revenue from the auction of import quotas accrues to general funds.

8.9. Collusion, conciliation and trade policy

Under appropriate conditions political candidates are therefore able to announce a trade policy formulated in terms of VERs that benefits both domestic and foreign interests. Such mutual producer benefit is not possible under a tariff. Hence the political advantage of the voluntary export restraint. It is possible to provide some gain to everybody—that is to say, everybody who matters by the criterion of sufficient political influence. The restriction of international trade can of course benefit foreign and domestic producer interests only at the expense of domestic consumers. Indeed, the VER turns the terms of trade against the trade-restricting economy.

The optimizing behavior of the political candidates gives rise to an announcement of a level of export restraint that trades off the interests of domestic and foreign producers. The equilibrium is a compromise between the trade policies sought by domestic and foreign producer interests. It is this compromise which makes the VER a politically appealing instrument of trade intervention. The tariff in contrast allows no compromise. Candidates adopt the extreme policy positions of either a prohibitive tariff or a zero tariff. The tariff is thus politically divisive, the voluntary export restraint politically conciliatory.

8.10. The political interest of the competitive fringe

VERs are a discriminatory trade restraint specifying the country of origin from which exports are specifically restrained. Competitive imports from other sources remain unconstrained. VERs are accordingly a source of a gain to competitive fringe exporters, via the increase in the domestic price in the export markets wherein the export restraints have been imposed. Competitive fringe exporters to the VER-restrained market thus have reason to favor restraints on exports by the dominant suppliers. Insofar as they exert political influence over the conduct of national trade policy, competitive fringe exporters thus have an incentive to use that influence to support the restriction of supply of their competitors via VERs.

8.4. Bibliographic notes

The model of domestic political competition, foreign interests and international trade policy which forms the core of this section is based on Hillman and Ursprung (1988). Husted (1986) documents the empirical evidence on outlays made by foreigners in the course of participation in the domestic political process. The foreign interest in the conduct of national trade policy has also been investigated by Das (1988) who considers the outcome of lobbying by domestic and foreign interests to influence protection in the form of an import quota. The collusive character of voluntary export restraints has been noted by Harris (1985), Eichenberger and Harper (1987) and Krishna (1988). Various aspects of the political economy of voluntary export restraints are noted in Jones (1984). On preemption and compensation, see Baldwin (1984), Bhagwati (1985) and Deardorrf (1987). Feenstra and Lewis (1987) identify the role of VERs in the formulation of incentive-compatible trade policies. For a model incorporating revenue seeking, see Brecher and Bhagwati (1987).

9. TRADE POLICY AS SOCIAL INSURANCE

The emphasis thus far has been on conflict of interest in the choice of trade policy. The conflict between gainers and losers from protection is predicated on known terms of trade. Given the terms of trade, protectionist policies change domestic relative prices and give rise to income-redistribution effects that advantaged individuals favor and disadvantaged individuals resist.

However, political endogeneity of trade policy need not imply conflict of interest. In the presence of uncertainty and with incomplete markets for risk sharing, there may on the contrary be a consensus favoring departure from free trade. Before the terms of trade are realized, individuals may not know if they will gain or lose from protectionist policies. It has been proposed that, confronted with this uncertainty, risk-averse individuals may have an incentive to agree to use trade policy as a form of social insurance. Rather than there being conflict over trade policy, collective choice can then yield consensus as ex-post redistributive commitments are made to maximize expected utility.

Or, rather than being formulated in terms of an objective of expected-utility maximization, trade policy has also been viewed as a means of redistributing income to maximize social welfare. Max Corden (1974) has for example proposed a "conservative social welfare function" as underlying the conduct of trade policy; the "conservative social welfare function" has the character that when used as a policy guide "the income of no significant group in the economy is allowed to fall by too much" as a consequence of trade-related change. Following any shift in comparative advantage, trade policy is viewed as applied to redistribute income in accordance with this income-preserving objective.

We have seen that such a view of government behavior in terms of a social-welfare-function objective is not necessary to explain policies that redistribute income to individuals whose incomes have declined as a consequence of shifts in comparative advantage. The political-support maximization model of policy choice as set out in Section 2 explains the use of trade policy as a redistributive device in terms of the self-interest of the policymaker, without recourse to the assumption of a benevolent government guided by social-welfare concerns.

The social-insurance perspective on endogenous trade policy does however offer a consensus alternative to the conflict-based vantage. The consensus outcome can be demonstrated in the context of a specific-factors model. In such a model, specific factor owners are in conflict on the course of trade policy for any given terms of trade that an economy might confront and mobile factor owners are subject to "the neo-classical ambiguity" (see Section 1); but ex-ante, before the terms of trade are realized, all undiversified factor owners, independently of their specialized source of factor income, may be able to increase their expected utility by agreeing to a protectionist policy if they are sufficiently risk averse. It can also be demonstrated that ex-post social welfare may be maximized by protection. The ex-ante consensus does not eliminate the ex-post conflict between gainers and losers from protection which has been the focus of the previous sections.

A case for governments using trade policy as a means of providing social insurance rests on the identification of a market failure that impedes the functioning of private insurance markets and a further demonstration that government intervention can be welfare-improving. However, of the types of market failure that might be used to justify a role for trade policy as social insurance— moral hazard, adverse selection, or imperfect observation of risky outcomes—none provide a theoretically adequate basis for a case for a social-insurance protectionist response. Thus, on basic theoretical grounds, trade policy as social insurance is compromised as a normative policy recommendation.

9.1. Risk aversion and social consensus

Consider the agents of the specific-factors model in a small trading economy confronting terms of trade variability. Let agents have undiversified claims to factor ownership, and assume an absence of insurance markets and markets for trades in claims to factor incomes. For owners of specific factors, price variability entails price uncertainty, since specific factors have no opportunities for ex-post adjustment when the terms of trade are realized. Mobile factors on the other hand have a natural form of insurance in that they optimize to maximize income by competitively adjusting sectoral employment when relative output prices change. Specific factors have for the reasons indicated in Section 1 well-defined self-interest stances on protection for any realized relative output price. The policy stance of mobile factors is ambiguous, reflecting the natural insurance afforded by opportunities for adjustment. Nonetheless, ex-ante, before the terms of trade are realized, all agents if sufficiently risk averse may find their expected utilities increased by a dampening of the variability of the ex-post distribution of relative prices. Reduced variability in relative-price realizations can be achieved via protectionist policies that are agreed upon ex-ante.

In the presence of relative price variability, use of the logarithm of relative price ensures results that are independent of the choice of numeraire. Hence, let $P \equiv P_1/P_2$ be the relative price of output, and define $z \equiv \ln P$. A risk-averse agent gains ex-ante from a mean-preserving reduction in the variability of income. The agent also gains from a reduction in the variability of relative price if utility is strictly concave in z. Express the utility of a representative individual i as $U^i(C_1^i, C_2^i) = V^i(P, y^i(P))$, where C_j^i is consumption of good j and y^i is real income. Variability of P affects V^i directly, and indirectly via $y^i(P)$. To express utility in terms of $\ln P$ (and suppressing the specific designation i of an individual), define $V = G[U^*(C_1, C_2)]$ where U^* is homogeneous of degree one and $G' > 0$. Let $I(P_1, P_2)$ be the minimum cost of achieving $U^* = 1$, where the price index I is homogeneous of degree one, strictly quasiconcave and strictly increasing. Then define $U^* = V^*(P_1, P_2, Y)$, where Y is nominal income. Given the linear homogeneity of U^*,

$$V = G(U^*) = G(V^*) = G\left[\frac{Y(P)}{I(P_1, P_2)}\right]. \qquad (9.1)$$

Normalize by setting $I(P_1, P_2) = 1$. Hence $P_2 I(P, 1) = 1$, and

$$P_2(z) = \frac{1}{I(e^z, 1)}. \qquad (9.2)$$

A distribution of the relative price P implies via (9.2) a distribution of the nominal price P_2.

Consider individuals who derive their incomes from undiversified ownership of a unit of a specific factor. Let $r_i(i = 1, 2)$ be the nominal (and using the normalization $I(P_1, P_2) = 1$ real) return of a specific factor. Via the link between specific factors' incomes and relative output prices, owners of factors specific to sector 1 gain from an increase in $P(\equiv P_1/P_2)$, and owners of factors specific to sector 2 lose. This is confirmed by substituting (9.2) into (9.1) and differentiating the resulting indirect utility function $V(z)$ to obtain

$$V'(z) = G' r_i'(P_2) \frac{dP_2}{dz} \begin{matrix} > 0, & i = 1 \\ < 0, & i = 2 \end{matrix}. \qquad (9.3)$$

However, for either type of specific factor owner,

$$\frac{1}{G'} V''(z) = \delta\left[r_i'(P_2)\frac{dP_2}{dz}\right]^2 + r_i''(P_2)\left(\frac{dP_2}{dz}\right)^2 + r_i'(P_2)\frac{d^2P_2}{dz^2}, \qquad i = 1, 2,$$
$$(9.4)$$

where $\delta \equiv G''/G'$ is absolute risk aversion. If $|\delta|$ is sufficiently great reflecting sufficient risk aversion, it follows that $V''(z) < 0$. Sufficiently risk-averse owners of specific factors can therefore gain ex-ante from trade restrictions that dampen the variability of the distribution of realized domestic prices.

Similarly, for mobile factors,

$$V(z) = G[w(P_2(z))] \qquad (9.5)$$

and

$$\frac{1}{G'} V''(z) = \delta \left[w'(P_2) \frac{dP_2}{dz} \right]^2 + w''(P_2) \left(\frac{dP_2}{dz} \right)^2 + w'(P_2) \frac{d^2P_2}{dz^2}. \qquad (9.6)$$

Mobile factors can either gain or lose ex-post from protection; consistently with the neo-classical ambiguity, $w'(P_2)$ in (9.6) can be positive or negative. However, in either case, if for owners of mobile factors $|\delta|$ is sufficiently great, then $V''(z) < 0$, and mobile factors also gain from a dampening of relative price variability.

State-contingent tariffs or quotas are means of reducing the ex-post variability of domestic relative output prices, and can thereby increase expected utility of all agents. Hence, the possibility arises of a social consensus for some departure from free trade.

The revenue from trade restrictions has not been included in the above formulation as a government transfer in specifying agents' incomes. The consensus possibility is thus sustained if the revenue is appropriated or dissipated. If the government does distribute the revenue from tariffs or sale of quota rights to domestic agents, there is a further benefit from protection beyond the gain via increased expected utility due to the reduction in the variability of realized relative output prices.

The expected gains from departure from free trade can be quite different for specific and mobile factors. There is in particular no presumption that risk aversion as expressed by δ in (9.4) and (9.6) is equal for different types of factor owners. In general therefore different departures from free trade will maximize the expected utilities of the different types of factor owners. The ex-ante consensus relates to the departure from free trade, but not necessarily the extent thereof.

There is of course commonality of interest with respect to the policy sought if all individuals are identical ex-ante, that is, if the commitment to a trade policy is made before individuals' claims over factors have been designated.

Deadweight losses are incurred in using the instruments of trade policy to dampen relative price variability. These losses would be avoided if risk-averse individuals were able to insure themselves directly against adverse realizations of the terms of trade.

It should be stressed that the gain from a commitment to depart from free trade arises here only ex-ante, in expected utility terms. There is uncertainty regarding the identification of the gainers and losers from protection. Agreement on some protection for those disadvantaged by the realization of the terms of trade offers partial insurance in the face of this uncertainty. Free trade however remains Pareto-efficient ex-post, and the conflicts among different factor owners regarding the conduct of trade policy are present in an ex-post equilibrium where the terms of trade are known.

9.2. Social welfare and ex-post income redistribution

The above view of trade policy as social insurance focuses on factor owners' expected utilities and the possibility of a consensus on trade policy when uncertainty regarding the terms of trade remains unresolved. While factor owners may gain in expected-utility terms from reduced relative price variability, ex-post incomes are left to be determined by the realization of the domestic relative price from the distribution of relative prices, as amended by the prespecified trade policy.

However, suppose that a government chooses trade policy after the realization of uncertain terms of trade to maximize social welfare. Again, consider the specific-factors setting. Let individuals initially have identical claims to a unit of capital, and also to a unit of mobile labor. Before the realization of the random terms of trade, each individual is obliged to allocate his capital indivisibly to one of two sectors. Hence, after the terms of trade have been realized, capital is sector-specific. Let there be two possible realizations of the terms of trade, P^A and P^B, where $P^A > P^B$ and $P \equiv P_1/P_2$. Individuals who have allocated their capital to sector 1 are therefore better off in state A than state B; and vice-versa for individuals who have allocated their capital to sector 2. In state i, an individual's income is

$$Y^i = r^{ij} + w^i + T^i \tag{9.7}$$

where r^{ij} is the rent in the sector j to which individual i has chosen to commit his capital, w^i is the state-contingent wage, and T^i is the state-contingent transfer of tariff revenue from the government. State contingent utility is

$$V^i = V[Y^i, P^i, (1 + t^i)] \tag{9.8}$$

where t^i is a state-contingent tariff levied on the numeraire (state-invariant) import good 2. In making capital allocation decisions under uncertainty, individuals equate expected utility across states of the world. Hence, denoting the probability of state i arising by ρ^i,

$$\sum_i \rho^i (V^{1i} - V^{2i}) = 0. \tag{9.9}$$

Let a proportion λ of individuals commit their capital to sector 1. Given λ, the government chooses a tariff to maximize

$$W = \sum_i \rho^i [\lambda V^{1i} + (1 - \lambda) V^{2i}]. \tag{9.10}$$

The tariff is therefore chosen ex-post in whichever state of the world is realized to maximize social welfare, which takes a Benthamite form.

Whether the tariff is anticipated or unanticipated, once the terms of trade are known social welfare can be increased by the use of trade policy to transfer income from low marginal utility of income to high marginal utility of income individuals. The prospect of social welfare improvement via such redistribution implies that individuals' utility functions are strictly concave in income; that is, in the face of terms of trade uncertainty individuals are risk averse.

Suppose that intervention is unanticipated. The allocation of capital to equate expected utilities across states of the world then implies anticipated realizations in state A of $V^{1A} > V^{2A}$ and in state B of $V^{2B} > V^{1B}$. A small tariff in the neighborhood of free trade changes social welfare according to

$$\frac{dW}{dt^i} = \lambda(1-\lambda)P^i(V_Y^{2i} - V_Y^{1i})\left[\frac{d(\Delta Yi)}{dt^i} + (C^{1i} - C^{2i})\right], \qquad i = A, B,$$

$$(9.11)$$

where $\Delta Y^i = (Y^{2i} - Y^{1i})$ and C^{2i} is state-contingent consumption of the import good. In state A, $V_Y^{2A} > V_Y^{1A}$ and $C^{1A} > C^{2A}$. From the properties of the specific-factors model, $d(\Delta Y^{1A})/dt^A > 0$. Hence, $dW/dt^A > 0$ so that a small state-A tariff is welfare improving. In state B, since $V_Y^{2B} > V_Y^{1B}$ and $C^{1B} < C^{2B}$, the sign of dW/dt^B is ambiguous. The ambiguity arises because in state B an import subsidy reduces the difference between marginal utilities of income, but the subsidy differentially benefits the high income group which consumes more of the import good. Which of the two countervailing effects dominates determines whether a tariff or an import subsidy achieves the state-B social-welfare maximizing income distribution.

If individuals anticipate the state-contingent policy response when assigning capital to the two sectors, social welfare is given by

$$W = \rho^A EV^A + \rho^B EV^B = EV. \qquad (9.12)$$

The government's objective of redistributing income to maximize social welfare is then equivalent to maximizing the expected utility of a representative individual before sectoral capital commitments have been made (and before the terms of trade have been realized). Again, a small positive tariff is welfare-improving in state A, and in state B either a tariff or an import subsidy is optimal.

State-contingent tariffs may not be feasible. In that event, the effect on social welfare of a small state-independent tariff in the neighborhood of free trade ($t = t^A = t^B = 0$) is given by

$$\frac{dW}{dt} = \lambda(1-\lambda)\sum_{i=A,B}\rho^i(V_Y^{2i} - V_Y^{1i})\left[\frac{d(\Delta Y^i)}{dt^i} + (C^{1i} - C^{2i})\right]. \quad (9.13)$$

The sign of this expression is ambiguous. Income is transferred from better-off to worse-off individuals via the effect of the tariff on consumer prices and via lump-sum redistribution of tariff revenue; but the change in producer prices transfers income from individuals who have allocated their capital to sector 1 to those who chose to allocate their capital to section 2. While this ambiguity is in principle present, Eaton and Grossman (1985) report that numerical simulations of this model reveal that a small positive state-independent tariff in general raises social welfare.

9.3. Ex-ante equality and ex-post redistribution

Figure 9.1 portrays the link between the ex-ante expected utility maximization and ex-post social welfare maximization approaches to trade policy as social insurance. For purposes of diagrammatic exposition, consider two identical individuals who confront the problem of indivisibly allocating their endowments of capital between two sectors before the realization of the terms of trade. In the absence of government intervention, the individuals choose allocations which maximize expected utility at E for the two possible realizations of the terms of trade yielding ex-post free-trade

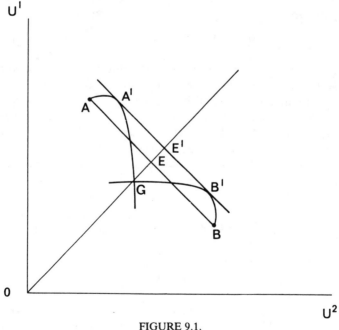

FIGURE 9.1.

outcomes at A and B. $AA'G$ and $BB'G$ are the respective state-A and B contingent utility possibility frontiers for redistribution via trade policy away from the free-trade income distribution. In state A the individual 2 who has allocated his capital to the revealed import-competing industry benefits from protection at the expense of individual 1 who has allocated his capital to the industry producing the good wherein the economy has been revealed to have a comparative advantage. Symmetrically, if state B eventuates, the tariff benefits individual 1 whose capital is then committed to the import-competing sector at the expense of individual 2. (Observe that in contrast with the rendition of section 9.2, comparative advantage here changes with the realization of the terms of trade.)

The argument of section 9.1 based on expected-utility maximization is that, if the individuals are sufficiently risk-averse, there can exist redistributions of income, achieved via the use of a tariff to dampen relative price variability, that yield expected utility in excess of the outcome at E. Thus, a tariff imposed on whichever turns out to be the import-competing good can transform the state-contingent outcomes A and B to respectively A' and B', yielding the higher expected utility at E'. The expected utility at E' is the maximal expected utility that can be achieved via the ex-ante social consensus to depart from free trade.

The realized outcome associated with E' is however either A' or B'. Ex-post, individuals do not achieve the same utility.

Suppose, however, that it were to be insisted that trade policy be used to provide complete insurance in the face of terms of trade uncertainty; so that, whichever state (terms of trade) is realized, individuals' ex-post utilities are to be identical. In the case depicted, this entails ex-post redistribution via trade policy to attain the equal distribution at G, beginning initially from either the free-trade outcome at A or that at B, depending on the realized terms of trade.

The common level of utility achieved in the complete insurance equilibrium at G is however less than expected utility at E (and E') because of the deadweight costs incurred in using the tariff to redistribute income. Expected utility at E' exceeds that at E because for small tariffs in the neighborhood of free trade the deadweight costs of protection are negligible. However, the deadweight cost becomes increasingly significant with higher tariffs.

Increasingly larger transfers are therefore required from the individual who has gained by committing his capital to the realized export sector to maintain the same marginal gain to the individual whose capital is committed to the import-competing sector.

Now, let the two individuals be called upon to decide on how trade policy is to be used to provide social insurance. Confronted with terms of trade uncertainty, the individuals choose the policy that maximizes expected utility. Hence, they prefer incomplete insurance at E' to complete insurance at G.

Expressed in terms of a Benthamite social welfare function, maximal welfare is also achieved ex-post at either A' or B' (depending on which state of the world has been realized), since the Benthamite social-welfare contours are straight lines with 45° slope.

The case in Figure 9.1 is not the necessary outcome of a comparison between ex-ante utility maximization and redistribution to ensure ex-post equality. If the deadweight costs of transferring income via the tariff were sufficiently small, the point E' could coincide with G (which would also coincide with A' and B'). A policy of providing full insurance by using trade policy to redistribute income ex-post subsequent to the realization of the terms of trade is then equivalent to the expected utility maximizing trade policy.

9.5. Technological uncertainty

A case for departure from free trade based on technological uncertainty has been made by Newbery and Stigltz (1984). The Newbery–Stiglitz model views domestic producers and consumers as distinct agents. Producers in two countries confront country-specific output uncertainty. There is however no uncertainty regarding aggregate world output. The only uncertainty is with regard to whether a country's producers will achieve a high or low realization of output. Given aggregate output, consumption preferences therefore specify an invariant free-trade price of output. Under free trade, producers confront income variability as a consequence of domestic output uncertainty. Autarky on the other hand stabilizes domestic producers' incomes, since producers are compensated for low realized outputs by high domestic prices.

Risk-averse producers therefore prefer autarky to free trade. Consumers may also prefer autarky, since producers confronting the uncertainty of the free-trade regime will be led by risk aversion to decrease planned output; hence under free trade less than optimal quantities of the risky good will be produced. The effect of country-specific uncertainty is thus equivalent to a tax on production of the risky good. Elimination of the uncertainty confronting domestic producers eliminates the distortionary effect of such a tax, albeit at the expense of foregoing the gains from trade.

It is clear that in the Newbery/Stiglitz model free trade is optimal ex-post. Once the distribution of output between countries has been realized, Pareto efficiency is achieved in the usual manner by using free trade to reach a consumption allocation on the contract curve. Any gain that derives from ex-post departure from free trade can only come via the effect on ex-ante production decisions of the commitment not to allow free trade ex-post. Direct income stabilization schemes break the link between producers' ex-ante input decisions and ex-post trade policy, and hence allow realization of the ex-post gains from international trade.

9.6. The anticipation of social insurance

The anticipation that governments will use trade policy as social insurance can of itself lead to inefficiencies in resource allocation. For example, suppose that firms anticipate intervention to preempt trade-related unemployment. Let firms perceive that the greater the number of workers who would be laid off in the event of an adverse shift in comparative advantage, the greater the likelihood of a protectionist response from government. Hence employees serve an insurance function for the firm, although imperfectly so, since there is no assurance of intervention. Suppose that a firm confronts a random world price for its output; let the price P_A arise with probability q_A and the price P_B with probability q_B, with $P_A < P_B$. Factor inputs are chosen before the price of output is realized. Capital is available at a competitive rental price r; but capital K once chosen is firm specific. The nominal wage for labor w, which is binding upon the firm and its employees, is contractually specified. However, the firm can change labor employment ex-post, after the realization of the price of output. In the event that the adverse price

P_B is realized, the firm fails to cover its variable costs and, unless the government intervenes, closes down laying off all its employees. Since the probability of intervention is perceived by the firm to increase with the number of workers who would be laid off, expected profits are

$$E\pi = q_A\pi_A + q_B[(1 - \rho(L))\pi_B + \rho(L)\tilde{\pi}_B] \qquad (9.14)$$

where $\rho(L)$ is the probability of intervention, π_A denotes profits in state-A, π_B denotes state-B profits if no intervention takes place, and $\tilde{\pi}_B$ denotes state-B profits if the government does intervene. Let $\pi_A = \tilde{\pi}_B$, so that intervention is state-B is a perfect substitute for the firm for a state-A outcome. Denoting state-A revenue by R_A, expected profits are

$$E\pi = [q_A + \rho(L)q_B](R_A - wL) - rK, \qquad (9.15)$$

and the firm's choice of capital and labor inputs is described by the conditions

$$[q_A + \rho(L)q_B]P_A F_K = r \qquad (9.16)$$

$$P_A F_L - w = -(R_A - wL)q_B\rho'(L)/[q_A + \rho(L)q_B] < 0. \qquad (9.17)$$

The condition (9.16) reveals that the firm is led by the dependence of ρ on L to increase its capital input choice, while (9.17) indicates that the firm employs more labor than called for by the equality of the wage and value of marginal product. The increased labor employment stems from the role of potentially unemployed labor in evoking social insurance-motivated protection. However, although increased labor employment is the means by which the firm makes a protectionist response more likely, anticipation of social insurance motivated intervention may lead the firm to choose more capital-intensive production techniques. Capital may be substituted for labor, since employment of capital, which is the risky input, is made more attractive by the increased likelihood of protection.

Whether production becomes more capital or labor-intensive, employment of both factors, is increased if the inputs are technological complements (i.e., $F_{KL} > 0$). Hence, output increases. Internalization of the likelihood of a social insurance-motivated policy response in adverse states of the world therefore gives rise to a protective expansionary effect on output.

There is adverse selection present, since firms confronting greater price variability have the greater incentive to avail themselves of the partial insurance provided by political sensitivity to unemployment. Political sensitivity to unemployment can be expected to be higher when a firm is the prominent employer of labor in a region. Firms confronting greater price variability thus have more to gain from being a principal regional employer of labor, which then increases the tendency for periodic local-unemployment "crises" to occur.

The anticipation of a social-insurance protectionist response gives rise to problems of time inconsistency in the formulation of trade policy. In a specific-factors setting, suppose that mobile labor once allocated to a sector can only be reallocated at a cost, and that the government maximizes a social welfare function wherein agents have weights proportional to the size of the group of factor owners to which they belong. A government implementing social-insurance motivated protectionist policies would wish to redistribute income ex-post, after the realization of the random terms of trade. However, suppose that the social-insurance protectionist response is anticipated. Then protection will have been internalized in factor allocation decisions. More factors will have been allocated to the import-competing sector than would have been the case, had a credible commitment to free trade been possible. In the time-consistent equilibrium, the protection provided is consistent with agents' anticipation of the social-insurance protectionist response. However, because of the time-consistency problem, protection motivated by social-insurance objectives is excessive, compared to the level of protection which would be provided could the social-welfare maximizing government credibly have announced a free-trade policy.

9.7. Market failures

Moral hazard, adverse selection and imperfect observability of the outcome of risky activities are causes of market failure that might underlie a social-insurance case for protection. Because of moral hazard, individuals may not be prepared to enter into commitments to share incomes derived from each other's human capital. Or via adverse selection high-risk individuals might drive low-risk individuals out of the market for pooling risks associated with undiversified factor holdings. Or the outcomes of risky activities may simply not be perfectly observable, hence again impeding risk-sharing arrangements. For any of these reasons, markets facilitating risk spreading of the returns to sector-specific human capital may not function efficiently. However, the presence of market failure in any particular instance does not of itself ensure that an improvement will be achieved via government intervention. Avinash Dixit has shown that none of the above considerations justify a protectionist social-insurance policy response.

Consider first moral hazard. In the presence of technological uncertainty, a competitive economy can allocate resources to produce either a riskless good y or a risky good x. The latter good has two possible output realizations, x_H (high) and x_L (low), which occur with respective probabilities $\rho(e)$ and $[1 - \rho(e)]$; e is the effort level in utility terms chosen by an x-sector worker, and effort influences the probabilities of the high and low output states arising via $\rho'(e) > 0$, $\rho''(e) < 0$. N risk-averse individuals allocate their labor services between the x and y sectors, and choose an effort level e before the realization of x. M workers choose to work in the safe sector and earn a wage $w = F'(M)$. The government can provide social insurance for individuals who have chosen to work in the x-sector via trade policy which establishes a domestic relative price different from the terms of trade $P = P_x/P_y$, or alternatively social insurance can take the form of direct net income transfers g_H and g_L to workers respectively realizing high and low outputs.

Effort levels affect only the probability with which a particular individual realizes one or the other of the outcomes, and not the values of the output realizations x_H or x_L. Were the realization of x to depend on e, contracts with appropriate penalties could account for moral hazard, since an individual's effort could be inferred from his realized x.

Individuals who have chosen employment in the risky sector decide upon a level of effort e to maximize expected utility,

$$EU_X = [1 - \rho(e)]V[I_L, P] + \rho(e)V[I_H, P] - e \qquad (9.18)$$

where I_L and I_H are the incomes respectively associated with low and high realizations of x. Incomes I_i are determined by an individual's realized output, together with government-provided social-insurance transfers g_H and g_L, private insurance transfers z_H and z_L, and a lump-sum tax t levied on all individuals, such that

$$I_i = Px_i + g_i + z_i - t, \qquad i = H, L. \tag{9.19}$$

The effort that maximizes expected utility (9.18) subject to income given by (9.19) satisfies

$$\rho'(e)[V(I_H, P) - V(I_L, P)] = 1, \qquad e > 0. \tag{9.20}$$

Now, impose an "exclusivity" requirement that all purchases of insurance by any individual be from the one competitive firm. The exclusivity assumption ensures that an individual's total insurance coverage is observed. A private insurance market outcome can be characterized by a competitively provided contract (z_H, z_L) which maximizes x-workers' expected utility (9.18), subject to a competitive zero-profit condition for the insurance industry and individuals' optimizing effort decisions satisfying (9.20). The private insurance contract internalizes moral hazard, since when choosing a contract (z_H, z_L) to offer an individual, firms are in effect determining the individual's effort level e (since via exclusivity an individual's choice of coverage is observed). The Lagrangean for the private competitive insurance contract is

$$\begin{aligned} L = &[1 - \rho(e)]V(I_L, P) + \rho(e)V(I_H, P) - e \\ &- \lambda_x\{[1 - \rho(e)]z_L + \rho(e)z_H\} \\ &+ \mu\{\rho'(e)[V(I_H, P) - V(I_L, P)] - 1\} \end{aligned} \tag{9.21}$$

with respective first-order conditions for choice of z_L, z_H, $e \geq 0$

$$[1 - \rho(e)][V_I(I_L, P) - \lambda_x] - \mu\rho'(e)V_I(I_L, P) = 0 \tag{9.22}$$

$$\rho(e)[V_I(I_H, P) - \lambda_x] + \mu\rho'(e)V_I(I_H, P) = 0 \tag{9.23}$$

$$\lambda_x\rho'(e)(z_L - z_H) + \mu\rho''(e)[V(I_H, P) - V(I_L, P)] = 0. \tag{9.24}$$

Dixit demonstrates that these conditions imply $z_L > 0 > z_H$; hence, although moral hazard is present, insurance though incomplete is nonetheless privately offered. Moreover, government intervention is ineffective. Beginning from an initial equilibrium with no social insurance, so that $g_L = g_H = 0$ and free trade prevails, neither direct transfers nor protection can increase the expected utility of an x-sector worker. Since in equilibrium $EU_x = U_y$, social insurance also does not affect the utility of a y-sector worker.

Maintaining exclusivity, let the economy confront aggregate risk. Then $\rho = \rho(e, \theta)$, where θ is a random variable. Conditional on θ, average output in the x-sector is riskless, and given by

$$\bar{x}(\theta) = [1 - \rho(e, \theta)]x_L + \rho(e, \theta)x_H. \qquad (9.25)$$

Again, the effort level e affects the probability that an individual will realize x_L or x_H, but not the values of these realizations. Hence θ can be inferred ex-post from (9.25), which allows ex-ante contracts to be conditioned on θ. Trade policy can therefore be specified as $p(\theta)$, and insurance via direct transfers as $g_L(\theta)$ and $g_H(\theta)$. Since the relative price of output P is now random, workers who choose employment in the y-sector also confront uncertainty.

The competitive private insurance contract $[z_L(\theta), z_H(\theta)]$ is now state-contingent. Let trade in contingent claims to purchasing power be feasible. The solution $[z_L(\theta), z_H(\theta)]$ which maximizes expected utility subject to the competitive zero-profit constraint for private insurance firms and individuals' optimizing effort decisions yields a constrained Pareto-efficient outcome. Beginning with free trade and no direct social-insurance transfers ($g_L(\theta) = g_H(\theta) = 0$ for any θ), small shifts of the functions $P(\theta)$, $g_L(\theta)$ and $g_H(\theta)$ cannot improve upon the expected utility achieved via competitively provided private insurance.

Exclusivity in insurance purchases permits monitoring of individuals' insurance purchases, which allows the private insurance market to internalize moral hazard, thereby yielding the efficient private insurance market outcome. However suppose that exclusivity is not possible. Let there be no aggregate risk, so that $\rho = \rho(e)$. With perfectly competitive insurance markets, an individual can trade $\alpha(e) = \rho(e)/[1 - \rho(e)]$ units of low-state income for one unit of high-state income. If z such contracts are purchased,

$$\begin{aligned} I_L &= Px_L + g_L - t + z\alpha(e) \\ I_H &= Px_H + g_H - t - z. \end{aligned} \qquad (9.26)$$

Expected utility is maximized by choice of z to equalize the marginal utility of income across states of the world, which implies $I_L = I_H$ and hence $V(I_L, P) = V(I_H, P)$. Insurance is therefore complete and $e = 0$. This complete-insurance/zero-effort equilibrium arises for whatever values of direct transfers (g_H, g_L) the government may choose and for any trade policy the government might adopt. Hence social insurance is also ineffective in the absence of exclusivity. The competitive private insurance market equilibrium conditional on the effort level chosen by optimizing individuals in Pareto efficient. However, while there is no indicated role for social insurance to replace or supplement private insurance, a tax on the purchase of insurance inhibits individuals' purchasing complete insurance, and hence induces individuals to choose a positive effort level.

Adverse selection fares no better as the basis for a case for social-insurance protectionist responses. In an informationally constrained Pareto-efficient equilibrium, let individuals confront world prices. Dixit (1987) shows that trade restrictions can only be welfare-worsening. A tax/subsidy policy which is directed at the specific externality that is the cause of market failure is the appropriate corrective policy. Taxes on international trade do not correct the adverse-selection market failure.

Trade policy may however be welfare-improving when the outcomes of risky activities are imperfectly observable. But when the risky good is imported, the appropriate policy is an import subsidy and not the import tax entailed in a protectionist social-insurance response.

9.8. Protection: Social insurance or political self-interest

The view of endogenous trade policy as reflecting social-insurance motives represents an alternative to political self-interest explanations of protectionist policies. The two explanations are quite different. Whereas the political self-interest vantage emphasizes conflict of interest, the social-insurance explanation emphasizes the possibility of social consensus; and whereas the political self-interest explanation focuses on income distribution as underlying protectionist responses, the social-insurance argument looks to efficiency grounds for intervention, justified by the failure of private insurance markets to facilitate pooling of trade-related risk. There is also an element of altruism in the social-insurance perspective. No binding contract ensures that those disadvantaged by shifts in comparative advantage will be the recipients of compensatory transfers from those who have been more fortunate. Compensatory payments are made because the fortunate are guided by the principle that "there but for good fortune go I."

Or alternatively the element of altruism is diminished if the principle is "there but for good fortune go I today, but who knows about tomorrow." That is, there may be a perceived value in precedent.

Scrutiny of the market-failure grounds for protectionist social-insurance responses demonstrates that incomplete markets for risk bearing do not imply a role for protectionist policies as social insurance. Hence, on efficiency grounds a case cannot be made for protection justified as social insurance. And we have observed that the very response associated with social insurance, protection provided to declining industries, is consistent with optimizing behavior by agents with policy discretion seeking to maximize political support. Further, not all declining industries are successful in evoking protectionist responses from government. Import-competing industries at times collapse—as proposed in Section 2 possibly because of political-economy benefit-cost calculations via the feedback from industry decline to loss of political influence. The differential success of declining industries in securing protection suggests that protectionist responses are better explained by idiosyncratic industry characteristics underlying the ability to influence political decisions than by a general social-insurance protectionist social safety net.

If indeed the motive for protectionist policies were to provide social insurance in the face of trade-related risk, one would expect there to be gains from the international pooling of such risk. International consensus should then be readily reached on the conduct of trade policy. Yet trade-policy negotiations tend to reflect conflicts of interest among countries rather than common risk-pooling motives. The political-economy perspective on trade policy explains the conflict among negotiating governments in terms of the political cost of making "trade concessions" that open up domestic markets to import competition.

9.8. Bibliographic notes

Second-best social-insurance aspects of protection have been noted by Corden (1974), Hillman (1977), Cassing (1980), among others.

The demonstration of social consensus on departure from free trade derived from expected utility maximization by risk-averse agents of the specific-factors model is based on Cassing, Hillman and Long (1986). The ex-post social-welfare maximization formulation of tariffs as insurance is from Eaton and Grossman (1985). Newbery and Stiglitz (1984) make the technological uncertainty argument for departure from free trade. The analysis of the effect on factor demand of anticipation of a social-insurance response to preempt unemployment is based on Hillman, Katz and Rosenberg (1987). Time-inconsistency aspects of protection provided by governments motivated by social-insurance objectives are considered by Staiger and Tabellini (1987). Dixit (1987a, 1987b, 1987c) investigates the market-failure foundations of the case for trade policy as social insurance. The observational equivalence of policymakers' behavior based on political-support maximizing objectives and considerations of social justice is noted in Hillman (1982). Political self-interest and social-insurance explanations for protectionist policies are compared in Hillman (1988).

10. THE INSTITUTIONAL SETTING

Trade policy decisions are made within an institutional setting that differs from country to country. For the developed countries, elements of a common institutional framework are provided by the General Agreement on Tariffs and Trade (GATT). The GATT also provides a forum for instituting change, via periodic multilateral rounds of negotiations on trade liberalization.

10.1. The General Agreement on Tariffs and Trade

The GATT sets out a code of conduct for the developed countries' trade policies. The intent of the Agreement is to promote liberalization of international trade. The GATT however lacks an enforcement mechanism and is not binding on national governments.

It was originally envisaged that the post world war II international institutional structure would include an International Trade Organization responsible for the conduct of trade policy. But the ITO, which was to have functioned alongside the International

Monetary Fund and the World Bank, never came into being. The ostensible reason is that national governments were not prepared to accept a role in the conduct of trade policy that was subordinate to an international organization. In particular, the U.S. Senate failed to ratify U.S. participation. Yet, although the attempt to institute a set of trading rules within the framework of the ITO was unsuccessful, agreement was reached in post world-war II negotiations on significant multilateral tariff reductions within the framework of the GATT.

The GATT differed from the proposed ITO in its institutional character. The ITO would have had "members". The GATT has "contracting parties" who agree to honor commitments made.

Various rounds of GATT negotiations have been successful in substantially decreasing levels of tariff protection in the developed countries. However, although exerting a liberalizing influence on world trade, the GATT has not succeeded in eliminating protection. Many tariff barriers that GATT negotiations have reduced or eliminated have been replaced by other tariffs and various non-tariff barriers which were outside the scope of GATT negotiations on liberalization.

The frame of reference adopted in GATT negotiations is instructive. GATT negotiations do not appear to be governed by the perspective on the gains from trade suggested by the welfare theorems of international trade theory. Rather, the negotiations presuppose the assignment of property rights to domestic market access to domestic producers. This assignment of rights is reflected in the terminology describing agreement on the liberalization of international trade. National governments make "concessions" in negotiations, in return for "concessions" made by foreign governments. The concessions qualify the rights of domestic producers to preempt foreign access to domestic markets. There is reciprocity. The concessions are granted in return for access to foreign markets granted to one's own domestic producers. Trade liberalization within the framework of the GATT thus takes the form of a qualified exchange of market access.

Domestic producers however retain their "rights". These rights are set out in the national trade laws of the contracting countries.

The GATT contract thus has two aspects. GATT negotiations

have facilitated multilateral liberalization of international trade. However, the GATT contract also institutionalizes a national property rights view of market access. From this latter prespective, as embodied in the national trade laws, the GATT contract sets out the rights of domestic producers to protection.

10.2. Administered protection: The national trade laws

The developed countries' national trade laws reflect in various degrees adherence to the articles of the GATT. The laws constitute a preexisting institutional framework for the presentation of protectionist pleas and formulation of protectionist responses, as distinct from activities directed at changing trade laws.

There are two routes that can be taken in the quest for protection. The national trade laws facilitate recourse to existing general legislation which specifies general technical criteria for intervention. The second route is to seek policy changes. Since this latter route entails persuading policymakers to introduce new legislation or alter existing policies, considerations of political influence and political support are central to the prospects for a successful protectionist response. The models of politically endogenous protection which view policymakers as balancing the political costs and benefits from intervention at the margin and which encompass lobbying and other influence-seeking activities are attempts to provide an analytical framework descriptive of this route to protection.

In the United States there are six administrative procedures that can facilitate protectionist responses within the context of existing legislation. These procedures have been summarized by Michael Finger (1988).

1) Escape clause or safeguards cases: These are investigations of 'injury' that a U.S. industry claims to have incurred because of import competition. Petitions are filed with the International Trade Commission, which investigates the domestic import-competing industry's claims. It is the ITC's responsibility to determine whether or not imports are the cause of injury to the petitioning industry. If the determination is affirmative, the ITC may recommend that the industry be provided 'relief' via tariffs or quantitative restrictions.

Or, rather than propose a protectionist response, the ITC may recommend adjustment assistance. The action taken is subject to executive discretion, which is in turn subject to Congressional override should the executive decide against protection when the ITC has so recommended, or should the executive choose a form of import restriction other than that proposed by the ITC.

2) Antidumping petitions: Such petitions are filed with the ITC, as well as with the International Trade Administration (ITA) of the Department of Commerce. Two investigations take place. A 'material injury' investigation is conducted by the ITC, and a sales at "less than fair value" investigation is conducted by the ITA. If both material injury and sales at less than fair value are confirmed, the Department of Commerce is required by law to impose antidumping duties. The antidumping law provides opportunities for an agreement to be reached between the petitioning domestic party and the foreign exporter whereby the foreign seller agrees to raise his price in the U.S. market. Such agreement is usually reached, since the foreign producer clearly prefers the price increase without duties to the price increase that would follow the imposition of duties.

3) Countervailing duty cases: As with dumping cases, so counter-vailing duty cases come under the auspices of the ITA, which conducts an investigation to determine whether foreign exporters are benefitting from subsidies provided by their governments. Generally an injury investigation is also conducted by the ITC. In affirmatively determined cases, the Department of Commerce is required by law to impose a countervailing duty equal to the net foreign subsidy. As with the antidumping law, the countervailing duty law allows for a case to be terminated upon agreement between the petitioning domestic party and the foreign exporter.

4) "Section 301": Under this law the President has the authority (1) to enforce U.S. rights under a trade agreement; (2) to respond to a foreign government's act of policy which is inconsistent with a trade agreement with the United States, or which denies benefits to U.S. interests under such an agreement; and (3) to react to activities or policies of foreign governments that are inconsistent with international obligations other than those arising under the GATT (for example, violations of a treaty of friendship, commerce and navigation). A complaint is brought by the U.S. firm

or industry to the Office of the U.S. Trade Representative which investigates to determine if the alleged violation has occurred. Section 301 cases often involve the interests of United States exporters. If the U.S. Trade Representative confirms the alleged violation, the President has the legal authority to take action against the offending party, including the imposition of import restrictions. Such "retaliation" is not limited to the particular product or service to which the foreign practice applied, but may be directed at any of the offending country's goods. Section 301 also requires the U.S. trade representative to activate GATT dispute settlement procedures, although the decision to retaliate is not tied to the GATT process. In practice, most 301 cases are settled by bilateral negotiations between U.S. and foreign governments. The part of the act concerned with "determination" of the existence of the offending activity appears directed at facilitating a negotiated settlement, by providing the President with the legal authority to impose sanctions if agreement is not reached.

5) Section 337: This section of the Tariff Act of 1930 declares unlawful import competition which might destroy or substantially injure a domestic industry, prevent the establishment of an industry, or restrain or monopolize trade and commerce in the United States. Most cases under this section involve patent infringement. Complaints are filed with the ITC, although the ITC can also investigate a suspected violation on its own initiative. Should the ITC determine that a violation has occurred, it may recommend that the foreigner not be allowed to sell his product in the United States. As with 301 cases, implementation of the ITC's recommendation is subject to executive discretion.

6) Section 406: Such cases concern market disruption due to imports from communist countries. Cases are decided by the ITC and sent to the President for final determination. The President's decision is subject to Congressional override should he reject or modify the ITC's recommendation.

Implicit in the above administrative procedures is the right of domestic interests to protection under specified circumstances. There is no specification of corresponding rights that might allow the losers from protection to protect their own interests. This is most evident in the safeguards or escape clause, which focuses only the injury incurred by a domestic industry as the consequence of import competition and makes no allowance for the offsetting gain secured by consumers and other users of the imported good. The fairness or unfairness of foreign trade practices is also not an issue in deciding whether a recommendation of protection is made.

The other five administrative procedures do identify foreign practices that are considered "unfair". However, although the conditions warranting the imposition of countervailing and anti-dumping duties are specified in the GATT, the identification of the circumstances wherein the conditions prevail takes place at the national level, and what is "fair" or "unfair" concerns only the effect of the trading practice on U.S. producers.

The administrative rules thus favor the gainers from protection. It is they who initiate procedures. The losers from protection cannot ask for levels of protection to be reduced. The losers have no rights set out in law and are provided with no forum to state their case—if the case would be made, given the problems associated with collective action encompassing a large number of beneficiaries and the related incentive for "rational ignorance" (see section 4).

The advantage of the gainers from protection on the administered track is tempered by executive discretion in acting upon ITC recommendations. The executive can decide against implementing an ITC recommendation, if a protectionist response is perceived to be contrary to "the national economic interests of the United States", or not in the "policy interest" of the United States. The conception of "national economic interest" is not that of gains from international trade. Michael Finger (1988) points out that, on the contrary, the executive often presents its case explaining why a protectionist recommendation has not been adopted by acknowledging that there is a cost borne by "the people" of the United States in not following through with a protectionist response. The "cost to the people" is presented as part of "the price of peace and political stability" associated with the achievement of foreign policy objectives. A basic point of discord in the conflict in the U.S. on the conduct of trade policy between the legislative and executive branches of government has been with regard to the extent to which domestic interests should be "sacrificed" for such foreign advantage.

A bias favoring liberal trade policy specifically emerges from the responsibility of the executive branch of government in assuring adherence to international trade obligations. In negotiations conducted within the framework of the successive rounds of the GATT, the U.S. has "surrendered" rights of domestic market access to foreign governments acting on behalf of their own producers. This contractual exchange of rights to market access is threatened by national protectionist policies. Executive discretion serves to assure the contractual "rights" of foreigners to domestic market access, rights which foreigners have secured, at "cost" to themselves, via their own "trade concessions".

10.3. The International Trade Commission

The International Trade Commission has a central role in the administrative procedures leading to protection. It is the interpretation of the evidence by the ITC which determines whether a protectionist proposal is made. In order to maintain an apolitical ITC, the members of the commission are appointed for a nine-year non-renewable term. The condition of non-reappointment and the nine-year duration are intended to provide incentives for members to make determinations and take positions that transcend short-term political interests. The intention is that ITC members should not perceive themselves as obligated to any particular political constituency, but should be free to investigate each complaint by a domestic import-competing industry on its merits with reference to the prespecified rules set out in the national trade laws.

ITC members are nonetheless political appointees, proposed by the executive and confirmed by the legislature. The appointees could reflect the policy disposition of the appointers. Robert Baldwin (1985) has studied the extent to which ITC members behave apolitically in their deliberations. Baldwin's findings support apolitical behavior, in that: "In making their decisions in import relief cases, the commissioners do not seem to be swayed by the views of Congress and the president on particular cases or by the ability of private interest groups to exert political power". On the other hand, Baldwin finds that determinations favoring the petitioning industry are more likely, the greater the industry's short-term (six-month) decline in profits and the greater the long-term (five year) decline in the industry's level of employment; whether short-term profits and long-term employment simultaneously declined was also significant in explaining the commissioners' decisions. These relationships are not inconsistent with the models of politically endogenous protection considered in previous sections. In particular, the relationships reflect the political appeal of declining industries as beneficiaries of protection. The legislative branch of government tends to be more sympathetic to protectionist pleas than the executive branch (see section 10.5). There is thus some significance to the report by Baldwin that: "An important finding . . . concerns the extent to which the Congress has influenced the nature of ITC appointments in recent years. By failing to confirm routinely presidential nominees to the commission, the Senate has forced recent presidents to nominate (to the ITC) more individuals who have had employment experience in Congress and the private sector rather than in the executive branch or academe". At the same time, investigating the ITC's record of decisions, Baldwin concludes that, in comparison with prior years when such influence by the legislative branch was less, "either a larger fraction of the cases brought before the commission in the 1975–1983 period were more deserving of an affirmative injury determination or the ITC has become more protectionist".

10.4. Political influence and administered protection

Escape-clause procedures involve executive discretion, whereas 'less-than-fair-value' cases (claims involving dumping and foreign subsidization) do not. Because of political discretion, the escape-clause or safeguards procedures of administered protection have been termed 'high-track', as distinct from the 'low-track' route provided by claims of less-than-fair-value.

   In principle, legal considerations dictate whether it is appropriate to seek administered protection via escape-clause or less-than-fair-value procedures: the former deals with injury from imports, the latter with the fairness or otherwise of the business practices adopted by foreigners. However, in practice, both procedures are directed at the same objective—protection. Finger, Hall and Nelson (1982) have proposed that which route will be effective in a quest for protection is founded in considerations of political influence rather than technical appropriateness. They suggest that: "Antidumping and countervailing duties are, functionally, the poor (or small) man's escape clause". And they add parenthetically that this poor man's escape clause "seems in a way to define comparative advantage as an unfair trade practice".

The high-track or escape-clause procedure has a political nature because the President is obliged to decide on how to act in the light of ITC recommendations. Baldwin (1985) found no relationship between the strength of support by ITC commissioners for a protectionist proposal and the executive decision regarding implementation, suggesting that independent considerations influence the exercise of executive discretion. In particular, the president, in deciding whether to proceed with an ITO recommendation, considers the likely public response to his decision.

Dumping and countervailing duty cases are determined subject to complex technical criteria as to what constitutes an unfair trade practice by foreigners. The predetermined criteria determine the validity of the plea for protection. A decision can be appealed in the Federal courts if a petitioner believes that the applicability of the technical criteria has been misinterpreted. No such right of appeal is provided for escape-clause determinations. Finger, Hall and Nelson view this as affirmation of the political nature of the escape-clause route, as compared to the technical character of 'less-than-fair-value' procedures.

Whether an industry takes the low or high-track administrative route to protection would thus appear to depend on the industry's political significance. A small industry can avoid the political forum by taking the technical track. A large industry with greater political visibility will with greater likelihood find itself confronting opposition to its protectionist pleas. Such opposition when expressed in the context of the complex technical criteria of dumping and countervailing duties cases will tend to make administrative determination intractable. By their nature, cases by highly visible or large petitioners will tend to become politicised, impeding progress via the technical administrative track.

Finger, Hall and Nelson confirm these predictions in a comparison between escape-clause and less-than-far-value cases for the years 1975 to 1979, the period during which the Trade Act of 1974 was in force. Variables characterizing technical considerations were statistically significant in explaining the outcome of less-than-fair-value cases, whereas variables characterizing political considerations tended to be statistically insignificant in such cases. The converse was true of escape-clause cases. Size in particular appeared to influence executive decisions in escape-clause cases. In cases where imports were in excess of $400m per annum an affirmative decision was made in five out of eight cases and the president acted to negotiate 'orderly marketing arrangements' in three cases; in smaller cases, only three out of seventeen decisions were affirmative, and no orderly marketing arrangements were negotiated.

10.5. The structure of government

The executive branch has been observed to have reasons for not automatically accepting protectionist recommendations made by the ITC, and the ITC itself although in principle but an interpreter of evidence and technical requirements is appointed by collaboration between the executive and legislature whose trade policy stances need not coincide. More generally, political agents occupying different positions in a governmental structure may confront different incentives to accept or reject protectionist pleas, whether such pleas entail interpretation of established rules or require the formulation of new trade policy. Political agents independently of their incentives may also differ in their abilities to influence trade policy.

Incentives derive from the character of a politician's constituency, and from the interests who are prepared to provide support (e.g. in the form of campaign contributions) to influence the voting behavior of the constituency. Thus, as noted, the President may see fit to override an ITC protectionist proposal that would benefit particular industry-specific interests because of broader national considerations; but also the President has a broad constituency. Since the President's constituency is all-embracing, the potential for political loss among constituents due to support for a narrow interest group is greater than in the case of a Senator, for whom in turn the potential for political loss among constituents is in general greater than of a member of the House. The geographic concentration of the beneficiaries of protection can thus be expected to influence trade policy.

A House member whose constituency includes a large concentration of gainers from a protectionist proposal accordingly has a greater incentive to support (or sponsor) the proposal than a Senator within whose state the House seat is located. Conversely, House members within whose constituencies concentration of gainers from protection is low will have little interest in supporting the protectionist proposal. Campaign contributions could however change the latters' positions, as could logrolling (agreements between legislators to trade votes on issues of little consequence for support on issues of importance).

The U.S. Senate has been observed in general to be more protectionist than the House. Because of relative concentration of the gainers and losers from a protectionist proposal, an individual senator may have less incentive to respond favorably to a special-interest protectionist plea than a member of the House. However, the rules governing conduct in Congress allow a senator greater ability to act. House procedures are less flexible and constrain individual initiative more than the rules of the Senate. In particular, the opportunities for introduction of protectionist legislation via the attachment of amendments to bills are greater in the Senate than in the House, where bills in general reach the floor from committee with little scope for change by individual House members.

The President, who given his broad constituency has the least incentive to support special-interest protectionist proposals, may nonetheless find it in his interest at times to adopt a protectionist position. The President has means of restricting imports that are not available to Congress. He can negotiate directly with foreign governments outside the framework of the GATT to secure 'voluntary' restraint of exports from countries which are causing 'injury' to domestic industry. Such executive intervention in general only occurs when recourse to other procedures has been unsuccessful. For example, 'voluntary' export restraints on Japanese automobiles were negotiated in 1981 only after recourse to the administrative trade laws had been unsuccessful, and after proposals had been initiated in Congress for the enactment of protectionist legislation.

As previously noted (section 7.2), besides automobiles, only textiles and apparel, steel, semiconductors, lumber, meat and sugar have been successful in having the executive negotiate trade restrictions on their behalf. However, these industries have in recent years accounted for approximately 25 percent of US imports.

Overall, the legislative branch of government has been more inclined to respond favorably to special-interest protectionist pleas than the executive branch. Hence proprotectionist interests would be predicted to seek to expand the scope of trade policy subject to the administrative rules and reduce the scope for executive discretion to override the rules. Consistently, changes in U.S. trade law as documented by Robert Baldwin (1985) have systematically narrowed the scope for executive discretion. In 1951 the Trade Act required that the President submit to Congress an explanatory statement if he chooses to reject an ITC protectionist recommendation. The 1958 Trade Act allowed Congress to override the President's rejection of an ITC recommendation by a two-thirds vote of the membership of each house of Congress. In 1962 the necessary vote for an override was reduced to a simple majority in each house, and in 1974 the override requirement was further reduced to a simple majority of members present in voting.

Bills before the Congress in 1987 proposed further containing the scope of presidential discretion to override protectionist proposals.

An example of the different positions often taken by the executive and the legislature in the U.S. is the presidential veto of the 1986 protectionist bill that had passed both houses of Congress with substantial support. A vote in the House to override the presidential veto fell short of the required two-thirds majority by only eight votes.

10.6. The motive for protection

The notion of "injury" that appears prominently in the trade laws may be perceived to reflect a social insurance motive underlying politically endogenous protection. Industry-specific interests "injured" by import competition may have wished to insure themselves against the contingency of such injury. With insurance markets absent, the administrative procedures available under the trade laws provide the policy-instituted substitute. On this view, the technically specified administrative rules governing protection set out the circumstances wherein the safety net provided by the national trade laws comes into play, and specifies the "remedies" in the face of "adversity" due to import competition.

However, this view of the motives for protection underlying the national trade laws is not supported by the scrutiny of the social-insurance justification for protection in Section 9, which suggested that the efficiency case for government intervention to redistribute income via protection is not firmly grounded in the theory of insurance-related market failures.

The administered-protection social safety net covers only trade-related injury, when an industry can just as well suffer "injury" because of a decline in domestic demand. The limitation of compensation under the trade laws to injury due to foreign competition can be tied to the property-rights conception of market access. The interpretation is that the trade laws assure domestic producers the preeminence specified by their rights in the home market and set out the allowable limits to foreign intrusion. Changes in domestic market conditions fall outside of this frame of reference as a source of "injury". Consistently, the administrative mechanism thus protects domestic industry interests from "injury" by foreigners.

10.7. Bibliographic notes

On GATT and the national trade laws, see Robert Baldwin (1980), John Jackson (1984), and Michael Finger (1986, 1988). On the different characters of the high and low tracks to administered protection in the U.S., see Finger, Nelson and Hall (1982). Baldwin (1985) provides a detailed analysis of the U.S. institutional structure within which U.S. trade policy is conducted. On the policy motives implicit in the national trade laws, see Hillman (1988).

11. EVIDENCE

There is considerable evidence supportive of the prediction of political-economy models that protectionist responses are endogenous to the political mechanism and derive from income-distribution rather than optimum-tariff, infant-industry, of second-best considerations. This section reviews the results of some empirical studies, both of the econometric and case-study type. The focus is on the U.S. The bibliographic notes provide references for additional studies for the U.S. and other countries.

11.1. From theory to empirically testable hypotheses

The theoretical models of politically endogenous protection imply empirically testable hypotheses about (1) the behavior of policymakers and (2) the relation between industry characteristics and levels of protection. With regard to policymakers, the models predict self-interested behavior directed at improving reelection prospects or at securing a share of the rents created via the contrived scarcity of imports. With regard to the beneficiaries of protection, the models predict that certain industry characteristics are conducive to achieving favorable protectionist responses from policymakers.

Observations on the behavior of policymakers and the characteristics of the beneficiaries of protection are provided by trade liberalization episodes. In the U.S. the authority to regulate international trade rests under the constitution with Congress (although the President has certain foreign policy prerogatives—see section 10). Thus, formally, Congress grants the President authority to engage in trade liberalization negotiations. For the purposes of participation in the Kennedy and Tokyo Rounds of multilateral tariff negotiations conducted under the auspices of the GATT, congressional authority was provided respectively by the Trade Expansion Act of 1962 and the Trade Act of 1974. For the Kennedy Round, the authority was to engage in negotiations to cut tariffs up to 50 percent and to eliminate altogether tariffs of less than 5 percent; for the Tokyo Round, the authority was to cut tariffs up to 60 percent with the same 5 percent elimination exception. Both the Kennedy and Tokyo Rounds of multilateral negotiations resulted in significant tariff reductions. The Kennedy Round yielded agreement on a 50 percent across-the-board cut in tariff levels. Tariff cuts for the Tokyo Round were based on a formula designed to achieve larger tariff reductions for larger tariff rates (the formula was $\Delta t/t = t/(t + 0.14)$, that is, tariffs of 14 percent were cut by precisely 50 percent, those above and below 14 percent by respectively more and less). However, those were the general rules. The political-economy perspective on endogenous tariff determination proposes that in the final analysis some industries will have fared better than others in resisting tariff cuts on competitive imports, or will have been successful in securing alternative forms of protection to compensate for decreases in levels of protective tariffs. The success of industries in resisting tariff reductions or in securing protection in alternative forms thus provides a test of the predictions of the political-economy model of trade-policy determination. An initial equilibrium will have been displaced by a reduction in the general level of protection. This comparative-statics change gives rise to a new equilibrium. A comparison between the pre- and post- trade liberalization equilibria establishes whether there were deviations from the general tariff-reduction rule for particular industries and, if so, permits an investigation of the characteristics of deviating industries to discern whether the deviations are consistent with the predictions of the political self-interest model of endogenous protection. At the same time, the trade-liberalization episodes provide observations on the behavior of policymakers in supporting or resisting liberalization, or in seeking exceptions to trade liberalization for certain industries.

11.2. Behavior by policymakers

Robert Baldwin (1985) has investigated the voting behavior of members of Congress on the 1974 Trade Act which authorized U.S. participation in the Kennedy Round. Baldwin hypothesized that the probability that a congressman would resist giving the President authority to liberalize trade would be greater, the more numerous were the beneficiaries of protection in his constituency and the greater were the campaign contributions received from protectionist interests. Baldwin also proposed that a congressman would be influenced in his voting behavior by the position taken by the President (in particular, if of his own party) and the congressional leadership of his party, in each case seeking to conform to these positions (ceteris paribus). Included in the regression equations were also variables such as incomes and skill levels characterizing the nature of the beneficiaries of protection. A congressman was further viewed as more likely to adopt a protectionist stance if such a position did not entail opposition to general liberalization of trade.

Analysis of the voting behavior of congressmen yielded outcomes consistent with the predictions of the political self-interest model of endogenous protection. Considerations of income distribution bearing upon elected official's constituencies were significant in explaining voting behavior. Baldwin concluded that: "the statistical analysis gives support to the hypothesis that in voting on trade-liberalizing legislation, members of Congress are sensitive to the import-competition problems of industries within their districts." The evidence also confirmed the importance of campaign contributions in influencing policymakers' behavior. A positive relationship was revealed between campaign contributions received from protectionist interests and the likelihood that a congressman would adopt a protectionist position.

11.3. Lame ducks and political victors

Interesting evidence on the motives of politicians in voting on trade-policy issues is presented by McArthur and Marks (1988), who examined voting on the domestic-content bill of 1982 which would have provided protection for domestic automobile components manufacturers. The congressional elections of 1982 preceded the vote on the protectionist bill. It was therefore possible to distinguish between congressmen who had been returned to office and those who had either been defeated or had not sought reelection (lame ducks). Ongoing congressmen were found to be more likely to vote in favor of the protectionist legislation than the lame ducks. An inference is that ongoing congressmen (successful continuing politicians) voted their political self-interest as dispensors of protection, whereas the lame ducks voted their interest as consumers or were influenced by broader national interests. McArthur and Marks interpret the evidence as indicating that "legislators with lower political opportunity costs were better able to resist protectionist pressures."

Relatedly, Tosini and Tower (1987) found in their analysis of voting on the 1985 textile bill that senators were more likely to take a protectionist position, the less time remaining until they faced election contests.

11.4. Changes in protection in the course of trade liberalization

The agreed rule for tariff reductions in the Kennedy Round was an across-the-board linear cut of 50 percent. The tariff reductions were implemented between 1968 and 1972, and international trade among the developed countries expanded. In the U.S., the ratio of imports to domestic production increased from 4.8 percent in 1967 to 7.3 percent in 1972.

The political self-interest perspective on determination of protectionist equilibria predicts a post-negotiation equilibrium differing in systematic ways from the negotiated uniform decline in protective tariffs. Industries with sufficient political influence should have been successful in defending their interests in the face of the negotiated decline in tariff barriers and to end up with levels of protection greater than consistent with a cross-the-board uniform reduction. One might also expect to see industries securing compensation for tariff reductions via non-tariff forms of protection.

These predictions are borne out in a study by Marvel and Ray (1983) of the pattern of U.S. protection which emerged subsequent to the Kennedy–Round negotiations. Industries which had characteristics conducive to exerting political influence to defend their interests were found to have succeeded in resisting tariff reductions in the face of overall liberalization. The liberalization of trade via the negotiated tariff reductions was also undermined by the introduction of new means of protection in the form of non-tariff barriers to international trade. Marvel and Ray proposed that the non-tariff barriers may well have increased the overall level of protection by more than the reduction in protection due to the lowering of tariffs.

Thus, notwithstanding the negotiated liberalization of trade via the reduction in tariff barriers, the historical patterns of tariff protection were maintained and new compensatory forms of protection were introduced as a response to the across-the-board tariff liberalization.

Marvel and Ray specified four industry-structure characteristics as proxies for the political influence that an industry might exert: (1) the industry's rate of growth, (2) industry concentration, (3) customer characteristics, and (4) comparative advantage.

The political self-interest model of protection (as set out in section 2) predicts that declining industries will, ceteris paribus, be beneficiaries of protection rather than industries that are expanding. The prediction is thus of a negative relationship between industry growth and protection.

Industry concentration is intended to reflect the organizational effectiveness of the industry coalition.

Customer characteristics are intended to capture the characteristics of the coalition opposed to industry protection. An industry with sales principally to consumers for final consumption confronts less cohesive opposition to protection than an industry whose sales are composed of intermediate inputs to other industries. The prediction is thus that consumer-goods industries will be more successful in resisting liberalization pressures.

The fourth industry characteristic, comparative advantage, reflects the industry's prospective gain from protection, and also considerations relating to reciprocity and retaliation. With U.S. comparative advantage identified to be in research and development intensive and advanced technology goods, the prediction is that increased technological sophistication of an industry's output will be reflected in greater loss of protection during the liberalization episode. Lowering of tariffs for those industries in whose output the U.S. exhibits a comparative advantage also facilitates negotiation of parallel reductions in foreign tariffs.

In the estimated regressions for tariff rates across industries, Marvel and Ray found all four variables to have the predicted signs and to be statistically significant. An industry's pre-liberalization level of tariff protection also contributed to the explanation of the post-liberalization tariff rates. That is, industries which had been successful in securing protection in the past remained so.

Tariffs and non-tariff barriers were revealed to be largely complementary: industries which benefitted from one form of protection also tended to benefit from the other. Tariff liberalization however led to substitution in the instrument of protection as non-tariff barriers were introduced to restore the protectionist political equilibrium in favored industries.

Consistently with the political-support maximization model of choice between tariffs and quotas (see Section 7.5), Marvel and Ray found non-tariff barriers to be more prevalent in low-concentration industries.

Robert Baldwin (1985) has also studied the relation between industry characteristics and outcomes of the Kennedy and Tokyo Rounds of trade liberalization. Tariff reductions were measured in terms of duties collected, and in terms of deviations of tariff reductions proposed by the U.S. (not the final outcome of the negotiations) from the Tokyo–Round tariff reduction formula. Baldwin found that the industries that had been more successful in resisting trade liberalization were characterized by unskilled low-wage employees, large numbers of workers, slow employment growth, high and rising import penetration ratios, and preexisting high levels of protection. The market-structure characteristics of numbers of firms in the industry and degree of industry concentration were not significant. Success in resisting liberalization pressures was greater, the greater the level of tariff protection that an industry had succeeded in achieving in the past and the higher the level of past protection achieved via non-tariff barriers.

Baldwin also investigated tariff reductions in a context allowing for simultaneity of demand for and supply of protection. The demand for protection was established according to whether an industry testified against the 1974 Trade Act during the House and Senate committee hearings on the bill. The supply of protection was reflected in the tariff reductions proposed by the U.S. for the Tokyo Round. Baldwin found that the intensity of demand for protection had a significant influence on ability to resist liberalization when the sample of industries was confined to those with tariff rates above 5 percent and when the measure of resistance to liberalization was the difference between the U.S. tariff-reduction offer and the tariff cut as established by the Tokyo Round formula. Unskilled labor, size of labor force and preexisting levels of protection were also important explanatory variables in determining an industry's success in resisting liberalization.

11.5. Trade liberalization and the developing countries

A study by Ray (1987) focuses on trade liberalization implemented under the Generalized System of Preferences (GSP) adopted in 1975 and the Caribbean Basin Initiative (CBI) of 1983. The GATT rounds of negotiations were aimed at liberalizing trade with the developed countries. The GSP and CBI were directed at reducing trade barriers confronting the developing countries' exports to the U.S.

Ray's study of the protectionist responses to the GSP and CBI suggests that U.S. import-competing industries were able to use their political influence to reregulate international trade to their advantage. The preferential trading agreement failed to offset any bias that may have been exhibited by U.S. protectionism against imports from the developing economies.

The Caribbean Basin Initiative was found to have been more effective than the GSP in liberalizing trade and establishing a pattern of international trade consistent with predicted comparative advantage. The CBI was adopted and implemented in haste following U.S. intervention in Granada. Ray proposes that the speed at which the CBI was implemented left U.S. domestic import-competing interests with little time to organize opposition via the political process. The domestic textile industry was however nevertheless able to protect itself from the trade liberalization effects of the CBI.

With regard to GSP, Ray found preferential status to be afforded primarily to products not subject to U.S. protectionist barriers. Highly protected domestic industries were not exposed to competition from GSP imports. Special-interest political-influence considerations appeared to override the broader liberalizing motives underlying the offer of preferential trading concessions to developing economies.

11.6. Industry characteristics and levels of protection: cross-sectional evidence

The trade-liberalization episodes offer evidence on changes in industries' levels of protection. The relation between industry characteristics and protection has also been investigated in the cross section, at a point in time.

Robert Baldwin (1985) has studied the cross-section pattern of pre-Tokyo Round tariff levels and non-tariff barriers. The results were broadly similar to the outcomes obtained with respect to industries' abilities to resist liberalization. Unskilled workers, low wages, and high labor value-added were found to characterize highly protected industries. The number of firms in an industry was also found to be significant in explaining levels of protection across industries: industries with fewer firms achieved higher levels of tariff protection. Again, tariffs and quota protection were related; industries which had secured high levels of tariff protection were also the beneficiaries of non-tariff barriers.

In another cross-section study, a model consistent with the political-support regulatory model has been formulated and tested by Paul Godek (1985). Policymakers were hypothesized to act in their self interest by maximizing a political-support function which trades off the interests of the gainers and losers from protection. Since trade policy can be used to political advantage to increase industry profits only by incurring the political cost associated with reduced consumer surplus, the political cost of using trade policy to redistribute income was specified to depend upon the rate of transformation between consumer surplus and industry profits. The transformation between consumer surplus and profits was the constraint subject to which policymakers maximized political support. Political support was hypothesized to depend on industry concentration, geographical concentration, the consumer/total sales ratio, and the average wage. Four measures of protection were employed; average tariffs, the presence or absence of a quota, the level of a quota index, and a total protection variable which encompassed measures of both tariff and quota protection.

The results of the regression analyses were interpreted to be consistent with the predictions of the political-support model of endogenous protection. As in other studies, the incidence of tariffs and quotas among industries was found to be positively correlated; industries which benefitted from tariff protection were also likely to benefit from quota protection. Quotas were however positively associated with high geographical concentration. Godek also found that the prominence of tariffs (the ratio of tariffs to total protection) declined across industries as total protection increased. At the margin, tariffs therefore became less important as the overall level of protection increased. Godek interprets the evidence as indicating that at high levels of protection quantitative restrictions are used to compensate foreigners for restriction of domestic market access, with quota rents going to foreigners via voluntary export restraints.

11.7. The U.S. timber industry: a case study

In January 1987 the Canadian government imposed a tax of 15 percent on exports of timber. The Canadian export tax protected the U.S. timber industry by increasing the U.S. domestic price of competitive Canadian timber. The export tax replaced an import duty that had been imposed by the U.S. government some months previously. The circumstances underlying this protectionist episode have been studied by Joseph Kalt (1988).

The U.S. lumber industry had in prior years been in decline. Imports from Canada had been increasing and domestic employment had been falling. The industry coalition—the Coalition for Fair Lumber Imports—had unsuccessfully petitioned for countervailing duties against Canadian softwood imports in 1982. The coalition's case was based on the claim that countervailing duties were justified by the Canadian government's subsidization of softwood lumber production, which materially injured U.S. lumber producers. Protection was however denied by application of a "general availability criterion," on the grounds that the subsidies reduced the cost of lumber to producers of a number of products beyond construction lumber—pulp and paper, plywood and veneer, furniture, turpentine, and food additives. However, shortly after the lumber decision, a "dominant use criterion" was evoked to justify protection of the U.S. steel industry against Brazilian steel made with subsidized iron ore. The Canadian lumber industry was the dominant user of Canadian trees. Hence a precedent was provided for a new protectionist petition by the U.S. industry. Faced with the prospect of a protectionist response by the legislature, the executive complied with the International Trade Commission's recommendation of a tariff, which was justified as countervailing the Canadian subsidy.

Political competition played a role in the executive's reversal of the earlier antiprotectionist position. The executive's protectionist decision preempted a protectionist response by Congress. Kalt notes that in the 1986 elections held subsequent to the protectionist decision, five Republican senators from lumber producing states were confronting reelection challenges.

Was Canadian lumber however indeed subsidized? A subsidy evokes an output response. However, rather than entailing a subsidy, the Canadian system of allocation of rights to fell trees could but entail the assignment of a rent to Canadian loggers, with no output response. Kalt points out that the right to fell trees is assigned administratively by the provincial forestry service in Canada, ostensibly independently of market conditions in the lumber market. Prices paid by loggers assigned rights to Canadian trees are substantially below the U.S. domestic price for like trees.

Canadian producers of lumber however purchased the trees from the loggers at the Canadian market price of timber, which did not differ substantially from the U.S. price. Thus, it would appear that the Canadian loggers may simply have secured a rent by virtue of the allocation of rights to trees. Since a rent has no output effect, there would then be no case for a countervailing duty.

An output response was however possible, since loggers could lobby to secure an increase in the amount of timber for which administrative permission would be given to cut.

Kalt conducted an econometric test to determine whether the Canadian stumpage subsidy evoked an output response, or was a rent established as a residual when the stumpage cost was subtracted from the market price of Canadian lumber. The results supported the proposition that the difference between the Canadian stumpage price for logs and the market price of timber was a rent rather than a subsidy. Hence, the evidence did not support a case for a countervailing U.S. duty.

The lumber protection episode accordingly provides an example of an instance where efficiency arguments were used to justify a protectionist response, but political-economy motives relating to rents and income distribution provided the apparent motivation for government intervention. Indeed, rather than correcting a distortion—due to the claimed foreign subsidization of an input into an export good—intervention created distortions via the protectionist measures adopted.

It remains to be considered why the U.S. insisted that the Canadian government replace the U.S. import duty on lumber with a Canadian export tax. This insistence resulted in the transfer of revenue from the U.S. Treasury to Canada. As Kalt notes, the U.S. started a trade war which it proceeded to lose: the U.S. monopsonistic tariff taking advantage of U.S. monopsony power with respect to Canadian lumber was replaced by a Canadian export tax exploiting Canadian monopoly power with respect to the U.S. market. The transfer of revenue to the Canadian government suggests compensation for the U.S. protectionist policy (see section 8.3). The losers from U.S. protection of the domestic timber industry were domestic U.S. consumers of lumber products and owners of factors specific to the Canadian timber industry. Compensation would imply that the revenue from the Canadian export tax ultimately reach the residual claimants in the Canadian timber industry. There is some evidence that this did happen, via a transfer of revenue from the Canadian federal government to the provincial authorities.

The ultimate losers from the U.S. lumber protectionist episode were therefore U.S. consumers of lumber products. U.S. producers gained from protection, and the Canadians were compensated for U.S. protectionism by the switch from a U.S. import duty to the Canadian export tax.

The U.S. government could claim that it had no choice but to respond to the Canadian subsidy. The Canadian federal government could in turn claim that, given the circumstances that it confronted, the best Canadian response was to implement the export tax thereby transferring the revenue to Canada. The U.S. government gained the political benefit associated with the protectionist response, while Canada gained the revenue.

Underlying the U.S. industry's claims of "unfairness" due to the Canadian subsidy was the Canadian prohibition of exports of logs to the U.S. The U.S. industry's argument was that it was denied access to "cheap" Canadian lumber. However, it would appear that the more appropriate claim is that U.S. interests were denied access to competition for the rents associated with assignment of rights to Canadian trees.

11.8. The U.S. steel industry: A case study

Robert Baldwin (1985) has provided a case study of protection secured by the U.S. steel industry using the political track to intervention. A further study by Gene Grossman (1986) has investigated the more recent circumstances of protection achieved by the steel industry using the administrative track to intervention.

In 1977, when the U.S. economy was in a recovery phase, the domestic steel industry found itself in difficulty. Imports were increasing and net income in the industry was falling. The industry blamed its plight on "unfair trading practices" of foreigners taking the form of foreign subsidies and dumping. Countervailing duties could however not be applied, since the U.S. government had waived the use of such duties during the course of negotiations that were taking place on a new international subsidies code. And although dumping charges had been filed, antidumping duties were regarded as undesirable by the administration because of the possibility of retaliation that would disrupt ongoing, multilateral trade negotiations (the Tokyo Round of the GATT).

To substantiate the steel industry's case, the American Iron and Steel Institute released a report confirming that the industry was being injured by foreign subsidies and unfair trading practices. This report evoked the release of a further study sponsored by the Japanese steel producers showing that the Japanese cost structure could not justify charges that Japanese steel was being dumped in the U.S. market. In the U.S., highly publicized closings took place of domestic plants, and workers who had been laid off staged demonstrations at the White House. The plant closings reduced the industry's profits via the associated write-offs of plant and equipment. Congress took heed of the industry's plight by calling for import quotas. A congressional steel caucus was formed with a membership of 25 senators and 125 members of the House, and the Senate passed a resolution calling for "vigorous enforcement" of unfair competition laws against foreign steel producers. The consequence of this political activity was the determination by the executive of a minimum price for steel imports. Import prices below the minimum price would be regarded as indicative of dumping.

For the most part, the minimum price was adhered to by foreign producers. For foreigners, the minimum price was preferable to the imposition of domestic duties, which would transfer rents from the restriction of trade to the U.S. government as revenue. The minimum-price provision was successful from the vantage of the U.S. industry. Baldwin reports that capacity utilization in the U.S. steel industry increased from 75 percent in December 1977 to 95 percent in May 1978. During the same period imports declined from 20 percent to 14 percent of domestic sales. The domestic industry had also secured a further benefit. Domestic firms had been able to close down technologically antiquated and unprofitable plants without incurring the wrath of layed-off workers; for the blame for the plant closings had been clearly placed with the unfair practices of foreign producers.

The minimum price set for imports of steel into the U.S. was subject to adjustment, to account for inflation. However, precisely because of inflation, the administration became reluctant in 1980 (an election year) to further raise the minimum import price. The U.S. industry responded by filing dumping charges in February 1980, and the administration responded by abandoning the minimum-price protectionist scheme. One month after the presidential election (which he had lost), the president reinstated the scheme at a minimum price 12 percent above the price prevailing when the scheme had been discontinued in March 1980. Limits were also set to the share of imports in domestic sales (an upper bound of 15.2 percent) and to capacity utilization in the domestic industry (a lower bound of 87 percent). The steel industry at the same time withdrew its dumping complaint.

This account demonstrates successful application of the political track to protection. Protection can also be secured via the technical track by recourse to the provisions of the national trade laws. As is often the case, the political track was here interwoven with the technical track.

Gene Grossman (1986) has studied a particular technical track appeal by the steel industry. In January 1984 Bethlehem Steel Corporation and the United Steel Workers of America filed a petition with the International Trade Commission seeking relief from imports under the escape-clause provision. The determination that protection was warranted would require establishing "serious material injury" to the steel industry, and that imports were "a substantial cause of that injury". The time period of the industry's petition was 1976–83. The ITC found in favor of the steel industry in June 1984.

Grossman conducted an econometric investigation aimed at establishing whether the ITC was correct in its finding that protection was warranted under the escape-clause provisions. His finding was that declines in employment in the U.S. steel industry were not principally explained by import penetration of the domestic market. Labor-saving changes in technology and declines in domestic demand were more significant contributing influences.

An important factor contributing to erosion of the international competitive position of the steel industry was the appreciation of the U.S. dollar. Exchange rate changes are not however included in the grounds for relief from import competition.

Grossman concludes that although the steel industry was successful in its plea for protection, study of the circumstances of the industry's difficulties reveals that the administrative criteria for protection were not satisfied. This parallels the conclusion reached by Kalt regarding the findings of the ITC with regard to the petition of the U.S. timber industry.

11.9. A long-run factor-proportions view

Steven Magee and Leslie Young (1987) have applied their model of political competition and endogenous protection (see section 4.5) to an explanation of long-run U.S. levels of protection. The period covered was 1905–1980. For each of 16 administrations, the level of tariff protection was calculated as the ratio of tariff revenue to the value of imports.

The long-run perspective proposed by Magee and Young is suggestive of a Heckscher–Ohlin or factor-proportions setting wherein factors are intersectorally mobile. Thus the gainers and losers from protection were identified as primary factors, capital and labor, rather than industry-specific interests. The U.S. labor/capital ratio was entered as an explanatory variable in the regressions, with an anticipated negative sign. The hypothesised negative relationship between levels of protection and the labor/capital ratio was based on the supposition that the U.S. tariff protected labor, increasing that factor's real income via the Stolper–Samuelsen Theorem and reducing the real income of capital. Over the period under consideration, the U.S. labor/capital endowment ratio had been falling. The Magee–Young model of political competition and endogenous protection predicts that an increase in the relative endowment of a factor of production will change the political equilibrium to that factor's advantage, since the resources and political influence of owners of the augmented factor will have increased (see section 4.5). The empirical results were mildly supportive of this prediction. The study reported the predicted negative relation between tariff levels and the labor/captial endowment ratio, but not a significant coefficient.

The regressions also included as an explanatory variable the industrial terms of trade of the U.S. The hypothesis was that deterioration in the terms of trade would be positively related to tariff levels, because of a 'compensation effect' associated with declining industries. Increased protection would compensate for adverse shifts in comparative advantage, as losers from terms of trade changes sought to protect their incomes via increased political activity. The losers here are owners of the relatively scarce domestic factor, who benefit from protection (not industry-specific interests, as in analyses of declining-industry protection). The empirical results confirmed the anticipated relationship between terms of trade changes and tariff levels.

The Magee–Young framework includes macroeconomic variables, target values of which are related to the political preferences of the party in power. Republicans are viewed as preferring low inflation at the expense of increased unemployment, Democrats as conversely preferring low unemployment at the expense of increased inflation. The predicted relation between the rate of inflation and the level of tariff protection was negative—when inflation increased, tariffs were hypothesised to fall, because in an already inflationary environment voter hostility to further protection-induced price rises would increase the political cost of protection. The predicted relation was confirmed in the regression analysis.

The introduction of macroeconomic variables leads Magee and Young to identify a "presidential party paradox". The paradox is that prolabor Democratic administrations tend to adopt liberal trade policies that are counter to the interests of the relatively scarce factor, labor; while conversely procapital Republican administrations tend to be more protectionist and thus adopt trade policies benefitting labor. Magee and Young propose that the paradox is resolved by viewing trade policy as derivative from macroeconomic policies. The preference of Democratic administrations for low unemployment and high inflation leads the U.S. dollar to weaken; whereas the Republican preference for lower inflation strengthens the dollar. Hence, greater protectionist pressures are generated under Republican administrations than under Democratic administrations. The 'protectionist party paradox' does not however reverse the political affiliations. Magee and Young propose that "labor is still better off economically under the Democratic administrations, because the Democratic freer trade effects will generally be dominated by Democratic prolabor macropolicy effects".

The Heckscher–Ohlin framework of the Magee–Young study which explains protection in terms of long-run factor-based interests stands in contrast with the dominant view and supportive evidence that protectionist pressures derive from industry-specific special interests.

11.10. Bibliographic notes

A number of studies have investigated political-economy explanations of protection in the developed economies. For further studies of the characteristics of U.S. protection, see Lavergne (1983) and Dougan (1984). Lavergne considers a number of hypotheses, one of which he terms the interest-group explanation for protection, but Lavergne's other hypotheses also encompass political-economy explanations of protectionist responses. Hufbauer, Berliner and Elliot (1986) report on 31 case studies of U.S. protection. Pincus (1975, 1977) investigates the pattern of protection in the antebellum United States. A historical political-economy based analysis examining the structure of tariffs across U.S. industries from 1870 to 1914 is provided by Baack and Ray (1983). On the political economy of U.S.–Japan trade in steel, see Patrick and Sato (1982). Anderson and Baldwin (1981) review the evidence from a number of World Bank country studies. On the EEC, see Verreydt and Waelbroeck (1982), on Germany Glismann and Weiss (1980), on Australia, Anderson (1980), on Canada, Caves (1976), Helleiner (1977), Saunders (1980). For surveys of the evidence presented in these studies, see Baldwin (1984, 1985). For a critique of aspects of the Magee–Young (1987) study, see Leamer (1987).

12. CONCLUDING REMARKS

Much of international trade theory has been prescriptive, directed at formulating policy proposals to present to policy makers. In the course taken by the modern theory at least up to the mid 1970's and then as subsequently pursued in a substantial part of the literature, free trade has been presented as the recommended trade policy, subject to qualifications deriving from the identification of various 'distortions' which underlie market failures. It has been commonplace to use the theoretical demonstration of the possibility of distortions and market failures to propound corrective interventionist policies. The policies are to be carried out by a benevolent omniscent planner who cares but for efficiency; or if income distribution is a concern for the omniscent planner, the theory allows him the use of lump-sum transfers (which do not disrupt factor-supply incentives) to maximize his conception of social welfare.

The social-insurance approach to trade policy as set out in section 9 is consistent with the market-failure perspective on policy. The approach suggests a second-best justification for governments' providing the trade-related insurance that individuals seek but which private insurance markets fail to offer.

Yet analysis of the market failures associated with the social-insurance case for intervention suggests that benevolent governments can do no better than achieve the efficiency outcomes obtained via privately organized markets. One may therefore wish to view income redistribution achieved via trade policy as reflecting charitable transfers to individuals disadvantaged by shifts in international comparative advantage. Altruism then explains trade policy, and the motives underlying trade policy are perceived as having to do with income-distribution objectives, not corrections of 'distortions' and the pursuit of efficiency objectives.

The literature reviewed in this monograph focuses on income-distribution motives as explaining the conduct of trade policy. However, rather than using notions of altruism or charity to explain protectionist policies, the literature views trade policy as deriving from a political process that allows individuals to pursue their self interests in seeking to influence policy outcomes. Policy choice is endogenous. No recommendations emerge for policymakers. Economic theory here is not advising policymakers how to formulate socially optimal trade policies. The theory is descriptive or positive. It seeks to explain observed protectionist outcomes and to predict the outcomes that emerge as individuals pursue their self interests in different circumstances.

A very basic source of difference between the omniscent-planner and the political-economy approaches to theories of international trade policy thus lies in the portrayal of government. The omniscent-planner formulations recognise no principal/agent problem between consumer/voters and policymakers. Governments are assumed to be perfectly benevolent agents of the individuals who compose society and are modelled as such. The political-economy models do not presuppose that a principal/agent problem necessarily exists. In certain circumstances the interests of the individuals who exercise policy discretion and the interests of consumer/voters may well coincide. But on the other hand the principal/agent problem is not assumed absent. And the political-economy models are consistent in integrating the optimizing behavior of individuals whose power is politically based with the optimizing behavior of economic actors. All individuals pursue their self interests, whether in government or without, and if in the context of political competition whether as incumbents or candidates for political office.

Section 5 and 6 focused on efficiency aspects of the endogenous determination of trade policy. It was observed that the use of resources to effect income transfers by influencing trade policy can be interpreted as socially wasteful (subject however to a qualification based on the 'distortions' literature). Again, the models here are descriptive. There is no associated inference that lobbying should be prohibited. On the contrary, the judgement can be made that lobbying is an essential part of the democratic process whereby individuals or groups with common interests seek to provide policymakers with information about policy preferences.

Nevertheless, it has been stressed that the incentive to lobby—and to actively provide political support—is often one-sided, with small groups securing advantage via the political process to the disadvantage of larger groups.

One may therefore conclude with a policy recommendation after all, that protectionist policy proposals be accompanied by independent evaluations (similar to 'environmental impact' statements) detailing the costs of protection to losers as well as the benefits to gainers. Given this information, one may wish to subject protectionist proposals to direct democracy; that is, individuals could be permitted to vote on whether they want protection for a particular good (and if so, the extent thereof, the duration, and the form).

Bibliography

Anam, Mahmudul (1982) Distortion triggered lobbying and welfare: A contribution to the theory of directly unproductive profit-seeking activities. *Journal of International Economics,* **13** 15–32

Anderson, Kym (1980) The political market for government assistance to Australian manufacturing industries, *Economic Record,* **56,** 132–144

Anderson, Kym and Robert E. Baldwin (1981) The political market for protection in industrial countries, Staff Working Paper no. 492, World Bank

Appelbaum, Eli and Eliakim Katz (1986) Rent seeking and entry, *Economics Letters,* **20,** 201–212

Appelbaum, Eli and Eliakim Katz (1986) Transfer seeking and avoidance: On the full social costs of rent seeking, *Public Choice,* **48,** 175–181

Appelbaum, Eli and Eliakim Katz (1987) Seeking rents by setting rents: The political economy of rent seeking, *Economic Journal,* **97,** 685–699

Axelrod, Robert (1984) *The Evolution of Cooperation,* New York: Basic Books

Baack, B. D. and Edward J. Ray (1983) The political economy of tariff policy: A case study of the United States, *Explorations in Economic History,* **20,** 73–93

Baldwin, Robert E. (1969) The case against infant-industry tariff protection, *Journal of Political Economy,* **77,** 295–305

Baldwin, Robert E. (1976) The political economy of postwar U.S. trade policy, *The Bulletin,* New York University Graduate School of Business

Baldwin, Robert E. (1980) The economics of the GATT, in Peter Oppenheimer, editor, *Issues in International Economics,* London: Oriel Press, 82–93.

Baldwin, Robert E. (1982) Tariff seeking and the efficient tariff: Comment, in Jagdish Bhagwati, editor, *Import Competition and Response,* Chicago: University of Chicago Press (for N.B.E.R.), 259–261

Baldwin, Robert E. (1982) The political economy of protectionism, in Jagdish Bhagwati, editor, *Import Competition and Response,* Chicago: University of Chicago Press (for N.B.E.R.), 263–286

Baldwin, Robert E. (1984) Rent seeking and trade policy: An industry approach, *Weltwirtschaftliches Archiv,* **120,** 662–677

Baldwin, Robert E. (1984) Trade policies in developed countries, in Ronald Jones and Peter Kenen, editors, *Handbook of International Economics,* Amsterdam: North-Holland, 571–619

Baldwin, Robert E. (1984) The changing nature of U.S. trade policy since World War II, in Robert E. Baldwin and Anne O. Krueger, editors, *The Structure and Evolution of Recent U.S. Trade Policy,* University of Chicago Press (for N.B.E.R.)

Baldwin, Robert E. (1985) *The Political Economy of U.S. Import Policy,* Cambridge, Mass: MIT Press

Becker, Gary S. (1983) A theory of competition among pressure groups for political influence, *Quarterly Journal of Economics,* **98,** 371–400

Becker, Gary S. (1985) Public policies, pressure groups and deadweight cost, *Journal of Public Economics,* **28,** 329–347

Bergstrom, Theodore, Lawrence Blume and Hal Varian (1986) On the private provision of public goods, *Journal of Public Economics,* **29,** 25–49

Bernholz, Peter (1966) Economic policies in a democracy, *Kyklos,* **19,** 48–80

Bernholz, Peter (1974) On the reasons for the influence on interest groups on political decision making, *Zeitschrift fur Wirtschafts und Sozialwissenschaft,* **94,** 45–63

Bernholz, Peter (1977) Dominant interest groups and powerless parties, *Kyklos,* **30,** 411–420

Bhagwati, Jagdish N. (1971) The generalized theory of distortions and welfare, in *Trade, Balance of Payments and Growth: Essays in Honor of Charles P. Kindleberger*, edited by J. N. Bhagwati, R. W. Jones, R. A. Mundell, and J. Vanek, North-Holland: Amsterdam, 69–90

Bhagwati, Jagdish N. (1980) Lobbying and welfare, *Journal of Public Economics*, **14**, 355–363

Bhagwati, Jagdish N. (1982) Directly unproductive profit-seeking (DUP) activities, *Journal of Political Economy*, **90**, 988–1002

Bhagwati, Jagdish N. (1985) Protectionism: Old wine in new bottles, *Journal of Policy Modelling*, **7**, 23–33

Bhagwati, Jagdish N. (1987) VERs, quid pro quo DFI and VIEs: Political-economy theoretic analysis, *International Economic Journal*, **1**, 1–14

Bhagwati, Jagdish N. and T. N. Srinivasan (1976) Optimal trade policy and compensation under endogenous uncertainty: The phenomenon of market disruption, *Journal of International Economics*, **6**, 317–336

Bhagwati, Jagdish N. and T. N. Srinivasan (1980) Revenue seeking: A generalization of the theory of tariffs, *Journal of Political Economy*, **88**, 1069–87

Bhagwati, Jagdish N. and T. N. Srinivasan (1982) The welfare consequences of directly unproductive profit-seeking (DUP) activities: Price versus quantity distortions, *Journal of International Economics*, **13**, 33–44

Brecher, Richard A. and Jagdish N. Bhagwati (1987) Voluntary export restrictions versus import restrictions: A welfare-theoretic analysis, in Henryk Kierzkowski, editor, *Protection and Competition in International Trade*: Essays in Honor of Max Corden, Oxford: Basil Blackwell

Brock, William A. and Stephen P. Magee (1978) The economics of special interests: The case of the tariff, *American Economic Review, Papers and Proceedings*, **68**, 246–250

Brock, William A. and Stephen P. Magee (1980) Tariff formation in a democracy, in John Black and Brian Hindley, *Current Issues in Commercial Policy and Diplomacy*, New York: St Martin's Press, 1–9

Buchanan, James M. and Gordon Tullock (1962) *The Calculus of Consent*, Ann Arbor: University of Michigan Press

Burgess, David F. (1980) Protection, real wages and the neo-classical ambiguity with interindustry flows, *Journal of Political Economy*, **88**, 783–802

Cassing, James H. (1980) Alternatives to protectionism, in J. Levenson and J. W. Wheeler, editors, *Western Economies in Transition*, Boulder: Westview Press, 391–424

Cassing, James H. (1981) On the relationship between commodity price changes and factor owners' real positions, *Journal of Political Economy*, **89**, 593–95

Cassing, James H. (1980) Alternatives to protectionism, in *Western Economies in Transition*, J. Levenson and J. W. Wheeler, editors, Boulder: Westview Press, 391–424

Cassing, James H. and Arye L. Hillman (1985) Political-influence motives and the choice between tariffs and quotas, *Journal of International Economics* **19**, 279–290

Cassing, James H. and Arye L. Hillman (1986) Shifting comparative advantage and senescent industry collapse, *American Economic Review*, **76**, 516–523

Cassing, James H., Arye L. Hillman and Ngo Van Long (1986) Risk aversion, terms of trade variability, and social-consensus trade policy, *Oxford Economic Papers*, **38**, 234–242

Cassing, James H., Timothy J. McKeown and Jack Ochs (1986) The political economy of the tariff cycle, *American Political Science Review*, **80**, 843–862

Caves, Richard E. (1976) Economic models of political choice: Canada's tariff structure, *Canadian Journal of Economics*, **9**, 278–300

Chamberlin, J. (1974) Provision of collective goods as a function of group size, *American Political Science Review*, **65**, 707–716

Cheng, Leonard (1987) Uncertainty and economic self-sufficiency, *Journal of International Economics*, **23**, 167–178

Coase, Ronald H. (1960) The problem of social cost, *Journal of Law and Economics*, **3**, 1–44

Colander, David C., editor (1984) *Neoclassical Political Economy: The Analysis of Rent-Seeking and DUP Activities*, Cambridge, Mass: Ballinger Publishing Company

Conybeare, John A. C. (1983) Tariff protection in developed and developing countries: A cross-sectional and longitudinal analysis, *International Organization*, **37**, 441–463

Corcoran, William J. and Gordon V. Karels (1985) Rent seeking behavior in the long run, *Public Choice*, **46**, 227–246

Corden, W. Max (1974) *Trade Policy and Economic Welfare*. Oxford: Clarendon Press

Coughlin, Cletus C. (1985) Domestic content legislation: House voting and the economic theory of regulation, *Economic Enquiry*, **23**, 437–448

Das, Satya P. (1988) Foreign lobbying and the political economy of protection, Department of Economics, Indiana University

Deardorrf, Alan V. (1987) Why do governments prefer nontariff barriers? *Carnegie–Rochester Conference Series on Public Policy*, Amsterdam: North Holland, **26**, 191–216

Deardorrf, Alan V. (1987) Safeguards policy and the conservative social welfare function, in Henryk Kierzkowski, editor, *Protection and Competition in International Trade*, Essays in Honor of Max Corden, Oxford: Basil Blackwell

Dixit, Avinash (1987) Trade and insurance with moral hazard, *Journal of International Economics*, **23**, 201–220

Dixit, Avinash (1987) Trade and insurance with adverse selection, Princeton University

Dixit, Avinash (1987) Trade and insurance with imperfectly observed outcomes, Princeton University

Dixit, Avinash (1987) How should the United States respond to other countries' trade policies? in Robert M. Stern, editor, *U.S. Trade Policies in a Changing World*, Cambridge, Mass.: MIT Press, 245–282

Dixit, Avinash and Victor Norman (1980) *Theory of International Trade*, Cambridge University Press

Dixit, Avinash and Victor Norman (1986) Gains from trade without lump-sum compensation, *Journal of International Economics*, **21**, 111–122

Dougan, William R. (1984) Tariffs and the economic theory of regulation, *Research in Law and Economics*, **6**, 187–210

Downs, Anthony (1957) *An Economic Theory of Democracy*, New York: Harper and Row

Eaton, Jonathan and Gene M. Grossman (1985) Tariffs as insurance: Optimal commercial policy when domestic markets are incomplete, *Canadian Journal of Economics*, **18**, 258–272

Eichenberger, Jurgen and Ian Harper (1987) Price and quantity controls as facilitating devices, *Economics Letters*, **23**, 223–228

Ethier, Wilfred J. (1984) Higher dimensional issues in trade theory, in Ronald W. Jones and Peter B. Kenen, editors, *Handbook of International Economics*, North-Holland, **1**, 131–84

Falvey, Rodney and Peter J. Lloyd (1986) The choice of the instrument of industry protection, in Richard N. Snape, editor, *Issues in World Trade Policy*, New York: Macmillan, 152–170

Feenstra, Robert C. (1984) Voluntary export restraints in U.S. autos 1980–1981: Quality, employment and welfare effects, in Robert E. Baldwin and Anne O. Krueger, editors, *The Structure and Evolution of Recent U.S. Trade Policy*, University of Chicago Press (for N.B.E.R.), 298–325

Feenstra, Robert C. (1985) Automobile prices and protection: The U.S.–Japan trade restraint, *Journal of Policy Modeling*, **7**, 49–68

Feenstra, Robert C. and Jagdish N. Bhagwati (1982) Tariff seeking and the efficient tariff, in Jagdish Bhagwati, editor, *Import Competition and Response*, University of Chicago Press (for N.B.E.R.), 245–258

Feenstra, Robert C. and Tracy R. Lewis (1987) Negotiated trade restrictions with private political pressure, NBER Working Paper no. 2374

Findlay, Ronald and Stanislaw Wellisz (1982) Endogenous tariffs, the political economy of trade restrictions, and welfare, in Jagdish Bhagwati, editor, *Import Competition and Response*, University of Chicago Press (for N.B.E.R.), 238–243

Findlay, Ronald and Stanislaw Wellisz (1983) Some aspects of the political economy of trade restrictions, *Kyklos*, **36**, 469–483

Findlay, Ronald and Stanislaw Wellisz (1986) Tariffs, quotas and domestic-content protection: Some Political-economy considerations, *Public Choice*, **50**, 221–242

Finger, J. Michael (1986) Comment on Tariffs, quotas and domestic-content protection: Some political-economy considerations, *Public Choice*, **50**, 221–242

Finger, J. Michael (1986) Ideas count, words inform, in Richard N. Snape, editor, *Issues in World Trade Policy*, New York: Macmillan, 257–280

Finger, J. Michael (1988) Protectionist rules and internationalist discretion in the making of national trade policy, in Hans-Jurgen Vosgerau, editor, *New Institutional Arrangements for the World Economy*, Springer-Verlag

Finger, J. Michael, H. Keith Hall and Douglas R. Nelson (1982) The political economy of administered protection, *American Economic Review*, **7**, 452–466

Frey, Bruno S. (1984) *International Political Economics*, Oxford: Basil Blackwell

Frey, Bruno S. (1985) The political economy of protection, in David Greenaway, editor, *Current Issues in International Trade*, London: Macmillan, 139–157

Frey, Bruno S., Werner W. Pommerehne, Friedrich Schneider and Guy Gilbert (1984) Consensus and dissention among economists: An empirical enquiry, *American Economic Review*, **74**, 986–994

Glismann, H. H. and F. D. Weiss (1980) On the political economy of protection in Germany, *World Bank*, staff working paper no. 427

Godek, Paul E. (1985) Industry structure and redistribution through trade restrictions, *Journal of Law and Economics*, **28**, 687–703

Gray, H. Peter (1975) Senile industry protection: A proposal, *Southern Economic Journal*, **41**, 538–541

Grossman, Gene M. (1983) Partially mobile capital: A general approach to two-sector trade theory, *Journal of International Economics*, **15**, 1–17

Grossman, Gene M. (1986) Imports as a cause of injury: The case of the U.S. steel industry, *Journal of International Economics*, **20**, 201–223

Grossman, Gene M. (1987) The employment and wage effects of import competition, *Journal of International Economic Integration*, **2**, 1–23

Grossman, Gene M. and J. David Richardson (1985) Strategic trade policy: A survey of issues and early analysis, Princeton University, International Finance Section, Special Papers in International Economics, no. 15

Grossman, Gene M. and James A. Levinsohn (1987) Import competition and the stock market return to capital, Discussion Paper no. 131, Woodrow Wilson School of Public and International Affairs, Princeton University

Guttman, Joel L. (1978) Understanding collective action: Matching behavior, *American Economic Review, Papers and Proceedings*, **68**, 251–255

Guttman, Joel L. (1985) Collective action and the supply of campaign contributions, *European Journal of Political Economy*, **1/2**, 221–241

Guttman, Joel L. (1987) A non-Cournot model of voluntary collective action, *Economica*, **54**, 1–19

Harberger, Arnold C. (1964) The measurement of waste, *American Economic Review*, **74**, 58–76; reprinted in A. C. Harberger, (1974) *Taxation and Welfare*, University of Chicago Press, 69–85

Harris, Richard (1985) Why voluntary export restraints are voluntary, *Canadian Journal of Economics*, **18**, 799–809

Hartigan, James C. and Edward Tower (1984) Tráde policy and the American income distribution, *Review of Economics and Statistics*, **66**, 452–458

Hartigan, James C., Philip R. Perry and Sreenivas Kamma (1986) The value of administered protection: A capital market approach, *Review of Economics and Statistics*, **68**, 610–617

Helleiner, G. K. (1977) The political economy of Canada's tariff structure: An alternative model, *Canadian Journal of Economics*, **10**, 318–326

Higgins, Richard S., William F. Shughart, and Robert D. Tollison (1985) Free entry and efficient rent seeking, *Public Choice*, **46**, 247–258

Hillman, Arye L. (1977) The Brigden Theorem, *Economic Record*, **53**, 434–446.

Hillman, Arye L. (1977) The case for terminal protection for declining industries, *Southern Economic Journal*, **44**, 155–160

Hillman, Arye L. (1982) Declining industries and political-support protectionist motives, *American Economic Review*, **72**, 1180–1187

Hillman, Arye L. (1988) Policy motives and international trade restrictions, in Hans-Jurgen Vosgerau, editor, *New Institutional Arrangements for the World Economy*, Springer-Verlag

Hillman, Arye L. (1988) The political economy of protectionism: Tariffs and retaliation in the timber industry: Comment, in Robert E. Baldwin, editor, *Trade Policy Issues and Empirical Analysis*, University of Chicago Press (for N.B.E.R.), 364–368

Hillman, Arye L. (1988) Tariff-revenue transfers to protectionist interests: Compensation for reduced protection or supplementary reward for successful lobbying? *Public Choice*, **58**, 169–172

Hillman, Arye L. and Eliakim Katz (1984) Risk-averse rent seekers and the social cost of monopoly power, *Economic Journal*, **94**, 104–110

Hillman, Arye L. and Eliakim Katz (1987) Hierarchical structure and the social cost of bribes and transfers, *Journal of Public Economics*, **34**, 129–142

Hillman, Arye L., Eliakim Katz and Jacob Rosenberg (1987) Workers as insurance: Anticipated government assistance and factor demand, *Oxford Economic Papers*, **39**, 813–820

Hillman, Arye L. and John Riley (1987) Politically contestable rents and transfers, presented at conference on *Political Economy: Theory and Policy Implications*, World Bank, Washington, D.C. In *Economics and Politics* (1989), **1**

Hillman, Arye L., and Dov Samet (1987) Dissipation of contestable rents by small numbers of contenders, *Public Choice*, **54**, 63–82

Hillman, Arye L. and Heinrich Ursprung (1988) Domestic politics, foreign interests, and international trade policy, *American Economic Review*, **78**, 729–745

Hirschleifer, Jack (1982) Evolutionary models in economics and law: Cooperation versus conflict strategies, *Research in Law and Economics*, **4**, 1–60

Hufbauer, Gary C., Diane T. Berliner and Kimberly A. Elliot (1985) *Trade Protection in the U.S.: 31 Case Studies*, Washington, D.C., Institute for International Economics

Hufbauer, Gary C. and Howard F. Rosen (1986) Trade policy for troubled industries, Washington, D.C.: Institute for International Economics

Husted, Steven (1986) Foreign lobbying and the formation of domestic trade policy, paper presented at the Western Economic Association Meetings, San Francisco

Jackson, John H. (1984) Perspectives on the jurisprudence of international trade *American Economic Review*, **74**, 277–281

Jones, Kent (1984) The political economy of voluntary export restraints, *Kyklos*, **37**, 82–101

Jones, Ronald W. (1971) A three factor model in theory, trade and history, in J. N. Bhagwati *et al.*, editors, *Trade, Growth and the Balance of Payments: Essays in Honour of C. B. Kindleberger*, Amsterdam: North-Holland, 3–21

Jones, Ronald W. (1975) Income distribution and effective protection in a multicommodity trade model, *Journal of Economic Theory*, **11**, 1–15

Jones, Ronald W. and Jose Scheinkman (1977) The relevance of the two-sector production model in trade theory, *Journal of Political Economy*, **85**, 909–935

Kaempfer, William H. (1986) Explaining the forms of protectionist policies: A public choice perspective, presented at Claremont-USC Conference on Blending Political and Economic Analysis of Internaitonal Trade Policies

Kaempfer, William H., J. Harold McClure, Jr., and Thomas D. Willett (1989) Incremental protection and efficient choice between tariffs and quotas, *Canadian Journal of Economics*

Kaempfer, William H., Steven V. Marks and Thomas E. Willett (1988) 'Why do large countries prefer quantitative restrictions?', *Kyklos*

Kaempfer, William H. and Thomas D. Willett (1989) Combining rent-seeking and public-choice theory in the analysis of tariffs vs quotas, *Public Choice*

Kalt, Joseph P. (1988) The political economy of protectionism: Tariffs and retaliation in the timber industry, in Robert E. Baldwin, editor, *Trade Policy Issues and Empirical Analysis*, University of Chicago Press for NBER, 339–364

Kalt, Joseph P. and Mark A. Zupan (1984) Capture an ideology in the economic theory of politics, *American Economic Review*, **74**, 279–300

Kalt, Joseph P. and Mark Zupan (1988) The apparent ideological behavior of legislators: Testing for principal-agent slack in political institutions, *Journal of Law and Economics*, **31**

Kau, James B., and Paul Rubin (1979) Self-interest, ideology and logrolling in congressional voting, *Journal of Law and Economics*, **22**, 365–384

Kemp, Murray C. (1962) "The gains from international trade," *Economic Journal*, **72**, 803–819

Kemp, Murray C., and Henry Wan Jr. (1986) Gains from trade with and without lump-sum compensation, *Journal of International Economics*, **21**, 99–110

Kindleberger, Charles P. (1951) Group behavior and international trade, *Journal of Political Economy*, **59**, 30–46

Krishna, Karla (1988) Trade restrictions as facilitating practices, *Journal of International Economics*

Krueger, Anne O. (1974) The political economy of the rent seeking society, *American Economic Review*, **64**, 291–303

Krugman, Paul R., editor (1987) *Strategic Trade Policy and the New International Economics*, Cambridge, Mass.: MIT Press

Lavergne, Real (1983) *The Political Economy of U.S. Tariffs: An Empirical Analysis*, New York: Academic Press

Leamer, Edward E. (1987) Comment on 'Endogenous Protection in the United States, 1900–1984', in Robert M. Stern, editor, *U.S. Trade Policies in a Changing World*, Cambridge Mass.: MIT Press, 196–200

Long, Ngo Van and Neil Vousden (1987) Risk-averse rent seeking with shared rents, *Economic Journal*, **97**, 971–985

Magee, Stephen P. (1980) Three simple tests of the Stolper–Samuelson Theorem, in Peter Oppenheimer, editor, *Issues in International Economics*, London: Oriel Press, 138–153

Magee, Stephen P. (1988) Optimal obfuscation and the theory of the second-worst: A theory of public choice, in S. P. Magee, W. A. Brock and L. Young, editors, *Endogenous Policy Theory*, Cambridge University Press

Magee, Stephen P. and William A. Brock (1983) A model of politics, tariffs and rent seeking in general equilibrium, in B. Weisbrod and H. Hughes, editors, *Human Resources, Employment and Development*, **3**, *Problems of Developed Countries and the International Economy*, Macmillan 497–523

Magee, Stephen P. and Leslie Young (1987) Endogenous protection in the United States, 1900–1984, in Robert M. Stern, editor, *Trade Policy in the 1980's*, Cambridge, Mass.: MIT Press, 148–195

Marvel, Howard P. and Edward J. Ray (1983) The Kennedy Round: Evidence on the regulation of international trade in the United States, *American Economic Review*, **73**, 190–197

Mayer, Wolfgang (1974) Short-run and long-run equilibrium for a small open economy, *Journal of Political Economy*, **82**, 955–967

Mayer, Wolfgang (1984) Endogenous tariff formation, *American Economic Review*, **74**, 970–985

Mayer, Wolfgang (1984) The political economy of tariff agreements, *Probleme und Perspektiven der Weltwirschaftlichen Entwicklung*, **5**, 423–437

Mayer, Wolfgang and Raymond G. Riezman (1987) Endogenous choice of trade policy instruments, *Journal of International Economics*, **23**, 377–381

Mayer, Wolfgang and Raymond G. Riezman (1987) Tariff formation in political-economy models, presented at conference on *Political Economy: Theory and Policy Implications*, World Bank, Washington D.C. In *Economics and Politics* (1989), **1**

McArthur, John and Steven V. Marks (1988) Constituent interest vs legislator ideology: The role of political opportunity cost, *Economic Enquiry*, **26**, 461–470

McGuire, Martin (1974) Group size, group homogeneity and the aggregate provision of a pure public good under Cournot behavior, *Public Choice*, **18**, 107–126

McKenzie, Richard B. (1986) Tax compensation schemes: Misleading advice in a rent-seeking society, *Public Choice*, **48**, 189–194

Mussa, Michael (1974) Tariffs and the distribution of income; The importance of factor specificity, substitutability and intensity in the short and long run, *Journal of Political Economy*, **82**, 1191–1203

Mussa, Michael (1978) Dynamic adjustment in the Heckscher–Ohlin–Samuelson model, *Journal of Political Economy*, **86**, 775–792

Mussa, Michael (1982) Imperfect factor mobility and distribution of income, *Journal of International Economics*, **12**, 125–141

Neary, Peter J. (1978) Short-run capital specificity and the pure theory of international trade, *Economic Journal*, **88**, 488–510

Nelson, Douglas R. (1981) The political structure of the new protectionism, *World Bank*, staff working paper no. 471

Newbery, David M. G. and Joseph E. Stiglitz (1984) Pareto inferior trade, *Review of Economic Studies*, **51**, 1–12

Olson, Mancur (1965) *The Logic of Collective Action*, Harvard University Press

Palda, Kristian S. (1975) The effect of expenditure on political success, *Journal of Law and Economics*, **18**, 745–771

Patrick, Hugh and Hideo Sato (1982) The political economy of U.S.-Japan trade in steel, in Cozo Yamamura, editor, *Policy and Trade Issues of the Japanese Economy*, Seattle: University of Washington Press

Peltzman, Sam (1976) Toward a more general theory of regulation," *Journal of Law and Economics*, **19**, 211–240

Peltzman, Sam (1984) Constituent interest and congressional voting, *Journal of Law and Economics*, **27**, 181–210

Pincus, Jonathan J. (1975) Pressure groups and the pattern of tariffs, *Journal of Political Economy*, **83**, 757–778

Pincus, Jonathan J. (1977) *Pressure Groups and Politics in Antebellum Tariffs*, New York: Columbia University Press

Pugel, Thomas A. and Ingo Walter (1985) U.S. corporate interests and the political economy of trade policy, *Review of Economics and Statistics*, **67**, 465–473

Ray, Edward J. (1987) The impact of special interests on preferential trade concessions by the U.S., *Review of Economics and Statistics*, **69**, 187–195

Ray, Edward J. (1981) Tariff and nontariff barriers to trade in the U.S. and abroad, *Review of Economics and Statistics*, 161–168

Ray, Edward J. (1981) The determinants of tariffs and nontariff trade restrictions in the U.S., *Journal of Political Economy*, **89**, 105–121

Ray, Edward J. and Howard P. Marvel (1984) The pattern of protection in the industrialized world, *Review of Economics and Statistics*, **66**, 452–458

Rodrik, Dani (1986) Tariffs, subsidies and welfare with endogenous policy, *Journal of International Economics*, **21**, 285–296

Ruffin, Roy and Ronald Jones (1977) Protection and real wages: The neo-classical ambiguity, *Journal of Economic Theory*, **14**, 337–48

Samuelson, Paul A. (1962) The gains from international trade once again, *Economic Journal*, **72**, 820–829

Samuelson, Paul A. (1971) Ohlin was right, *Swedish Journal of Economics*, **73**, 365–384

Saunders, Ronald S. (1980) The political economy of effective protection in Canada's manufacturing sector, *Canadian Journal of Economics*, **13**, 340–348

Staiger, Robert and Guido Tabellini (1987) Discretionary trade policy and excessive protection, *American Economic Review*, **77**, 823–828

Stigler, George (1971) The theory of economic regulation, *Bell Journal of Economics*, **2**, 3–21

Stigler, George (1972) Economic competition and political competition, *Public Choice*, **13**, 91–106

Stigler, George (1974) Free riders and collective action: An appendix to theories of economic regulation, *Bell Journal of Economics and Management Science*, **4**, 359–365

Stolper, Wolfgang and Paul Samuelson (1941) Protection and real wages, *Review of Economic Studies*, **9**, 58–73

Takacs, Wendy E. (1981) Pressures for protectionism: An empirical analysis, *Economic Enquiry*, **19**, 687–693

Tosini, Suzanne C. and Edward Tower (1987) The textile bill of 1985: The determinants of congressional voting patterns, *Public Choice*, **54**, 19–25

Tullock, Gordon (1967) The welfare costs of tariffs, monopolies and theft, *Western Economic Journal,* **5,** 224–232

Tullock, Gordon (1980) Efficient rent seeking, in J. M. Buchanan, G. Tollison and G. Tullock, editors, *Toward a Theory of the Rent Seeking Society,* Texas A&M Press 97–112

Tullock, Gordon (1971) The cost of transfers, *Kyklos,* **24,** 629–643

Tullock, Gordon (1984) Long run equilibrium and total expenditures in rent seeking: A comment, *Public Choice,* **43,** 95–97

Verreydt, Eric and Jean Waelbroeck (1982) European Community protection against manufacturing imports from developing countries; A case study in the political economy of protection, in Jagdish Bhagwati, editor, *Import Competition and Response,* University of Chicago Press (for N.B.E.R.), 369–393

Viner, Jacob (1929) The Australian tariff, *Economic Record,* **5,** 306–315

Wallerstein, Michael (1987) Collective bargaining and the demand for protection, *American Journal of Political Science,* **31,** 729–752

Wellisz, Stanislaw and John D. Wilson (1986) Lobbying and tariff formation: A deadweight loss consideration, *Journal of International Economics,* **20,** 367–375

Young, Leslie (1982) Endogenous tariffs, the political economy of trade restrictions and welfare: Comment, in Jagdish Bhagwati, editor, *Import Competition and Response,* University of Chicago Press (for N.B.E.R.), 238–243

Young, Leslie and Stephen P. Magee (1986) Endogenous protection, factor returns and resource allocation, *Review of Economic Studies,* **53,** 407–419

INDEX

FUNDAMENTALS OF PURE AND APPLIED ECONOMICS

SECTIONS AND EDITORS

BALANCE OF PAYMENTS AND INTERNATIONAL FINANCE
W. Branson, Princeton University
DISTRIBUTION
A. Atkinson, London School of Economics
ECONOMIC DEVELOPMENT STUDIES
S. Chakravarty, Delhi School of Economics
ECONOMIC HISTORY
P. David, Stanford University, and M. Lévy-Leboyer, Université Paris X
ECONOMIC SYSTEMS
J.M. Montias, Yale University
ECONOMICS OF HEALTH, EDUCATION, POVERTY AND CRIME
V. Fuchs, Stanford University
ECONOMICS OF THE HOUSEHOLD AND INDIVIDUAL BEHAVIOR
J. Muellbauer, University of Oxford
ECONOMICS OF TECHNOLOGICAL CHANGE
F.M. Scherer, Harvard University
EVOLUTION OF ECONOMIC STRUCTURES, LONG-TERM MODELS, PLANNING POLICY, INTERNATIONAL ECONOMIC STRUCTURES
W. Michalski, O.E.C.D., Paris
EXPERIMENTAL ECONOMICS
C. Plott, California Institute of Technology
GOVERNMENT OWNERSHIP AND REGULATION OF ECONOMIC ACTIVITY
E. Bailey, Carnegie-Mellon University, USA
INTERNATIONAL ECONOMIC ISSUES
B. Balassa, The World Bank
INTERNATIONAL TRADE
M. Kemp, University of New South Wales
LABOR AND ECONOMICS
F. Welch, University of California, Los Angeles, and J. Smith, The Rand Corporation
MACROECONOMIC THEORY
J. Grandmont, CEPREMAP, Paris

MARXIAN ECONOMICS
J. Roemer, University of California, Davis
NATURAL RESOURCES AND ENVIRONMENTAL ECONOMICS
C. Henry, Ecole Polytechnique, Paris
ORGANIZATION THEORY AND ALLOCATION PROCESSES
A. Postlewaite, University of Pennsylvania
POLITICAL SCIENCE AND ECONOMICS
J. Ferejohn, Stanford University
PROGRAMMING METHODS IN ECONOMICS
M. Balinski, Ecole Polytechnique, Paris
PUBLIC EXPENDITURES
P. Dasgupta, University of Cambridge
REGIONAL AND URBAN ECONOMICS
R. Arnott, Boston College, Massachusetts
SOCIAL CHOICE THEORY
A. Sen, Harvard University
STOCHASTIC METHODS IN ECONOMIC ANALYSIS
Editor to be announced
TAXES
R. Guesnerie, Ecole des Hautes Etudes en Sciences Sociales, Paris
THEORY OF THE FIRM AND INDUSTRIAL ORGANIZATION
A. Jacquemin, Université Catholique de Louvain

FUNDAMENTALS OF PURE AND APPLIED ECONOMICS

PUBLISHED TITLES

ISSN: 0191-1708